ACTS

Chapters 1—14

J. Vernon McGee

THOMAS NELSON PUBLISHERS

Nashville

Published in Nashville, Tennessee, by Thomas Nelson, Inc., and distributed in Canada by Lawson Falle, Ltd., Cambridge, Ontario.

Scripture quotations are from the KING JAMES VERSION of the Bible.

Library of Congress Cataloging-in-Publication Data

McGee, J. Vernon (John Vernon), 1904–1988
 [Thru the Bible with J. Vernon McGee]
 Thru the Bible commentary series / J. Vernon McGee.
  p.   cm.
 Reprint. Originally published: Thru the Bible with J. Vernon McGee. 1975.
 Includes bibliographical references.
 ISBN 0-8407-3291-0
 1. Bible—Commentaries. I. Title.
BS491.2.M37 1991
220.7′7—dc20
                                        90-41340
                                        CIP

Printed in the United States of America
1 2 3 4 5 6 7 — 96 95 94 93 92 91

CONTENTS

ACTS—Chapters 1—14

PREFACE

The radio broadcasts of the Thru the Bible Radio five-year program were transcribed, edited, and published first in single-volume paperbacks to accommodate the radio audience.

There has been a minimal amount of further editing for this publication. Therefore, these messages are not the word-for-word recording of the taped messages which went out over the air. The changes were necessary to accommodate a reading audience rather than a listening audience.

These are popular messages, prepared originally for a radio audience. They should not be considered a commentary on the entire Bible in any sense of that term. These messages are devoid of any attempt to present a theological or technical commentary on the Bible. Behind these messages is a great deal of research and study in order to interpret the Bible from a popular rather than from a scholarly (and too-often boring) viewpoint.

We have definitely and deliberately attempted "to put the cookies on the bottom shelf so that the kiddies could get them."

The fact that these messages have been translated into many languages for radio broadcasting and have been received with enthusiasm reveals the need for a simple teaching of the whole Bible for the masses of the world.

I am indebted to many people and to many sources for bringing this volume into existence. I should express my especial thanks to my secretary, Gertrude Cutler, who supervised the editorial work; to Dr. Elliott R. Cole, my associate, who handled all the detailed work with the publishers; and finally, to my wife Ruth for tenaciously encouraging me from the beginning to put my notes and messages into printed form.

Solomon wrote, ". . . of making many books there is no end; and much study is a weariness of the flesh" (Eccl. 12:12). On a sea of books that flood the marketplace, we launch this series of THRU THE BIBLE with the hope that it might draw many to the one Book, *The Bible*.

J. VERNON McGEE

The

ACTS

of the Apostles

INTRODUCTION

The Book of Acts, sometimes called the fifth Gospel, is a continuation of the Gospel of Luke. Dr. Luke is the writer, as he states in his introduction (v. 1). Sir William Ramsay, after making a critical study of Luke's writings, declared that Luke was the greatest historian, ancient or modern.

The Book of Acts is remarkable in many ways. It is a bridge between the Gospels and the Epistles. The New Testament without the Book of Acts leaves a great yawning gap. As Dr. Houston puts it, "If the book of Acts were gone, there would be nothing to replace it." The last recorded fact about Jesus in the Gospel of Matthew is the Resurrection, which is recorded in Acts 1. In the Gospel of Mark, the last recorded act of Jesus is the Ascension, which is also recorded in Acts 1. In the Gospel of Luke, the last recorded fact is the promise of the Holy Spirit. That is also in Acts 1. And in the Gospel of John the last recorded fact is the second coming of Christ. You guessed it—that is also in Acts 1. It is as if the four Gospels had been poured into a funnel, and they all come down into this jug of the first chapter of the Book of Acts. Also the great missionary commission, which appears in all four Gospels, is confirmed in the Book of Acts.

The Book of Acts furnishes a ladder on which to place the Epistles. It would be an enriching experience to read them together, as Acts gives the history of the founding of the churches to which the Epistles are directed.

The Book of Acts records the beginning of the church, the birth of the church. The book of Genesis records the origin of the spiritual body which we designate as the church.

The theme or key to the Book of Acts is found in 1:8: "But ye shall receive power, after that the Holy Ghost is come upon you: and ye shall be witnesses unto me both in Jerusalem, and in all Judaea, and in Samaria, and unto the uttermost part of the earth."

The book divides naturally according to this key verse. The first seven chapters record the Lord Jesus Christ at work by the Holy Spirit through the apostles in *Jerusalem*. Chapters 8 through 12 record the Lord Jesus Christ at work by the Holy Spirit through the apostles in *Judea* and *Samaria*. The remainder of the book is devoted to the Lord Jesus Christ at work by the Holy Spirit through the apostles unto the *uttermost part of the earth*.

The Book of Acts is not complete. It breaks off with Paul in his own hired house in Rome. It has no proper ending. Do you know why? It is because the Book of Acts is a continuing story. Perhaps the Lord has Dr. Luke up there writing the next chapters now. Perhaps he is recording what you and I do for Christ in the power of the Holy Spirit. I hope so.

Some special features of the Book of Acts are:

1. Prominence of the Lord Jesus Christ. The Lord Jesus has left His disciples now. He is gone. He has ascended in the first chapter of the book. But He is still at work! He has just moved His position, His location. He has moved His headquarters. As long as He was here on this earth, His headquarters were in Capernaum. Now His headquarters are at the right hand of the Father. The Lord Jesus Christ is prominent. He is at work from the vantage place of heaven itself.

2. Prominence of the Holy Spirit. Christ promised to send the Holy Spirit. This promise is mentioned in the Gospel of John four times (John 1:33; 7:37–39; 14:16–17; 20:22). The same promise is given in the Book of Acts (Acts 1:8). You and I are living in the age of the Holy Spirit. The great fact of this age is the indwelling of the Holy Spirit in believers.

3. The power of the church. There is a power in the church and, of course, this is the working of the Spirit of God. That power of the early church is not manifested in churches today. Why? Because the early church operated on a high spiritual level which has not again been attained in any age since then. However, it is the Holy Spirit working through the believer when any service brings honor and glory to the Lord Jesus Christ.

4. Prominence of the church, visible and invisible. The church is a new institution. It has come into existence in the Book of Acts.

5. Prominence of places. The book begins at Jerusalem and ends in Rome. Sir William Ramsay checked all the places mentioned by Dr. Luke and found them to be accurate.

6. Prominence of persons. Dr. Luke mentions 110 persons by name, besides the references to multitudes or crowds. I believe that by the end of the first century there were millions of believers in the world. The church had a phenomenal growth in those first two to three hundred years. It certainly has slowed down today, exactly as our Lord said it would.

7. Prominence of the Resurrection. The Resurrection is the center of gospel preaching. In too many churches today, we have one Easter sermon once a year. As a pastor, many times I have featured Easter in August. People would come just to find out what had happened to the preacher. They thought the heat was getting to me. However, in the early church the resurrection of Jesus Christ was the very center and heart of the message, and no sermon was preached without it. The theme of Peter on the Day of Pentecost was the resurrection of Jesus Christ. He explained that what was taking place on that day was because of the fact that Jesus was now in heaven at the right hand of God and had sent His Holy Spirit into the world. It was all due to the Resurrection. You will find that the Resurrection is the very heart of the messages of Paul.

There are a great many people and preachers who like to "ride a hobby." Some people like to ride the hobby of prophecy; others dwell on the Keswick message or some other facet or phase. Now, if you want to ride a hobby, let me suggest one for you: the resurrection of Jesus Christ. In the early church, every Sunday was Easter, a day to proclaim the Resurrection. "He is risen!" was proclaimed everywhere (see Matt. 27:64).

8. There is a prominence of Peter in the first section of the book and of Paul in the last section. There is a strange omission of the other apostles. God had good reasons, I am sure, for emphasizing the ministry of these two men.

Also there is a human reason. I believe that Dr. Luke was acquainted with the ministries of these two men. He was an associate of Paul. Some people hold the idea that there was a disagreement between Peter and Paul. Very candidly, I am of the opinion that Dr. Luke and Peter and Paul got together a great many times and had many talks.

The proper title for this historical book has always been a problem. The Bible which I use is the authorized version, and there it is called *The Acts of the Apostles*. The Codex Vaticanus and the revised versions also call it *The Acts of the Apostles*. Robert Lee called it *The Acts of the Ascended and Glorified Lord*. The Bantu title is *Words Concerning Deeds*.

I would rather think that the key is given to us in the first two verses of the first chapter. On the basis of this, I would venture a title which is a rather long one: *The Lord Jesus Christ at Work by the Holy Spirit through the Apostles*.

OUTLINE

I. **The Lord Jesus Christ at Work by the Holy Spirit through the Apostles in Jerusalem, Chapters 1—7**
   A. Preparation for the Coming of the Spirit, Chapter 1
      1. Introduction, Chapter 1:1–2
      2. Forty Days Post-Resurrection Ministry of Jesus, Chapter 1:3–8
      3. Ascension and Promise of the Return of Jesus, Chapter 1:9–11
      4. Waiting for the Spirit, Chapter 1:12–14
      5. Appointment of an Apostle, Chapter 1:15–26
   B. Day of Pentecost
      (Bethlehem of the Holy Spirit), Chapter 2
      1. Coming of the Holy Spirit, Chapter 2:1–13
      2. First Sermon in the Church Age of Peter, Chapter 2:14–47
   C. First Miracle of the Church; Peter's Second Sermon, Chapter 3
      1. Healing of Lame Man, Chapter 3:1–11
      2. Appealing and Revealing Address of Peter, Chapter 3:12–26
      3. Believing Five Thousand Men (Results), Chapter 4:4
   D. First Persecution of the Church; Power of the Holy Spirit, Chapter 4
   E. Death of Ananias and Sapphira; Second Persecution, Chapter 5
   F. Appointment of Deacons; Witness of Stephen, a Deacon, Chapter 6
   G. Stephen's Address and Martyrdom (First Martyr), Chapter 7

II. **The Lord Jesus Christ at Work by the Holy Spirit through the Apostles in Judea and Samaria, Chapters 8—12**
   A. Conversion of Ethiopian Eunuch (Son of Ham), Chapter 8
   B. Conversion of Saul of Tarsus (Son of Shem), Chapter 9

CHAPTER 1

THEME: Preparation for the coming of the Spirit

As suggested in the Introduction, in my opinion the proper title for the Book of Acts would be: *The Lord Jesus Christ at Work by the Holy Spirit through the Apostles.* And the first seven chapters reveal the Lord Jesus Christ at work by the Holy Spirit through the apostles in Jerusalem. The first chapter, which is the preparation for the coming of the Holy Spirit, includes a brief introduction; a resumé of the forty-day post-resurrection ministry of Jesus; His ascension and promise of return; then the apostles waiting for the Spirit, and their appointment of an apostle to take the place of Judas.

INTRODUCTION

The former treatise have I made, O Theophilus, of all that Jesus began both to do and teach,

Until the day in which he was taken up, after that he through the Holy Ghost had given commandments unto the apostles whom he had chosen [Acts 1:1–2].

The "former treatise" was Luke's gospel, which also was directed to *Theophilus*—whose name means "lover of God." I totally reject the idea that just any lover of God is intended. Obviously Luke knew a man by the name of Theophilus, and undoubtedly the name was appropriate—a lover of God. Luke's gospel was "all that Jesus began both to do and teach," and in the Book of Acts Jesus *continues* to do and to teach. Today He is still at it, if I may use that expression, and He will continue on with this present program until He takes His own out of the world.

"Until the day in which he was taken up, *after that* he through the Holy Ghost [Spirit]" makes it clear that just because Jesus was taken up into heaven didn't mean He ceased doing and teaching. But now, from the vantage place of the right hand of God, He is continuing to work through the Holy Spirit. As in the army where commands pass from one man to another, so the Lord Jesus Christ is working through the Holy Spirit; the Holy Spirit operates through the apostles and on out to you and to me where we are today. This is a remarkable statement here.

FORTY DAYS POST-RESURRECTION MINISTRY OF JESUS

Dr. Luke uses one of his periodic sentences here, which continues on through verse 4.

To whom also he shewed himself alive after his passion by many infallible proofs, being seen of them forty days, and speaking of the things pertaining to the kingdom of God [Acts 1:3].

He showed Himself alive by many *infallible* proofs after His suffering and death. There are ten recorded appearances of Jesus after His resurrection. His post-resurrection ministry, as revealed in His appearances, has a more important bearing on the lives of Christians today than does the three-year ministry recorded in the Gospels. I have a little book entitled *The Empty Tomb*, which tells of this post-resurrection ministry of the Lord Jesus. Paul stated it this way: "Wherefore henceforth know we no man after the flesh: yea, though we have known Christ after the flesh, yet now henceforth know we him no more" (2 Cor. 5:16).

You and I do not know Him today as the One who walked on this earth over nineteen hundred years ago. We know Him as the one Man in the glory. He is up there right this moment, and He is real. How often the church loses sight of this fact.

Recently a letter came to me from a person who said he had been a church member all his life. He had gone through all the prescribed rituals, and he thought he was a Christian. Then through hearing the

Word of God, he learned that he didn't even know Jesus. The wonderful discovery for him was that not only did Jesus walk on this earth nineteen hundred years ago, but also He is alive today and is sitting at God's right hand. He came to the living Christ and received Him as Savior and Lord. How wonderful that is! Jesus showed Himself alive by many infallible proofs.

The problem of the unbeliever today is not with the facts but with his own unbelief. The facts are available. I wonder whether anyone doubts that the Battle of Waterloo was an historical event. Very frankly, I believe that Napoleon lived, and I believe that he fought the Battle of Waterloo. But I have very little evidence for it. Actually there is ten thousand times more evidence for the death and resurrection of the Lord Jesus Christ than there is for the Battle of Waterloo, and yet there are people today who say they do not believe it. Where is the problem? The problem is in the heart, the unbelieving heart. There is a natural tendency for man to run away from God just as Adam did. Man turns his back upon God today. If you are an unbeliever, the problem is with you. The problem is not in the Word of God. He showed Himself alive by many infallible proofs. You can know if you really want to know. The problem is that you don't want to know. The problem is not in the mind; the problem is in the will.

Let me insert a comment here about the Resurrection. There is a verse which I think has been twisted and distorted. The Lord Jesus Christ said, "And I, if I be lifted up from the earth, will draw all men unto me" (John 12:32). How was He lifted up? He was lifted up in the Resurrection, friend, lifted up from the dead. That is the message. Regardless of how much you talk about Jesus or how lovely you say that He is, the message is that He has been lifted up from the dead. He is risen! The reason that more people are not drawn to Christ is that there is not the preaching of a resurrected Christ. How the Book of Acts puts the emphasis on the resurrection of Jesus Christ!

And, being assembled together with them, commanded them that they should not depart from Jerusalem, but wait for the promise of the Father, which, saith he, ye have heard of me [Acts 1:4].

That's the end of the sentence—these first four verses are all one sentence! The apostles are to wait for the coming of the Holy Spirit. Until that event takes place, His command is to wait.

> **For John truly baptized with water; but ye shall be baptized with the Holy Ghost not many days hence [Acts 1:5].**

The risen Jesus appeared to the apostles and gave them these instructions. He tells them that something is going to happen to them. They are going to be baptized with the Holy Spirit not many days hence. This baptism of the Holy Spirit is the promise of the Father, and Jesus had previously told them about it.

It is very important to point out that this is not talking about water baptism, which is *ritual* baptism. This is the baptism with the Holy Spirit. The baptism of the Holy Spirit is *real* baptism. It is this baptism of the Holy Spirit which places a believer into the body of believers, which we sometimes refer to as the church.

When we get to the second chapter, which tells of the coming of the Holy Spirit on the Day of Pentecost, we will learn that they were filled with the Holy Spirit. Filling was necessary in order that they might serve. The fact that they were filled with the Holy Spirit for service indicates that the other ministries of the Holy Spirit had been performed.

> **When they therefore were come together, they asked of him, saying, Lord, wilt thou at this time restore again the kingdom to Israel? [Acts 1:6].**

You will find that some of the commentators rebuke the apostles for asking this question—they feel the apostles made a mistake. I believe that the answer the Lord gives them indicates they made no mistake. Their question was a legitimate question, a natural question, and one that our Lord answered as such. He did not rebuke them. He did not call it a foolish question.

The apostles were brought up and schooled in the Old Testament.

They had waited for the coming of the Messiah. They understood that the Messiah is the One who will establish the kingdom upon this earth. That was their hope. It is still the hope for this earth. God is not through with this earth. God does not intend to sweep this earth under the rug. Although it is small enough to be swept under His rug, He is not going to do that. God has an eternal purpose for the earth. It was the kingdom of God that they talked about, which involves the re-establishment of the house of David. These were the things He talked about after His resurrection—we see in verse 3 that He spoke of things "pertaining to the kingdom of God."

And he said unto them, It is not for you to know the times or the seasons, which the Father hath put in his own power [Acts 1:7].

He let them know, at this particular time, that the kingdom would not be established. Rather, He would call out a people to His name, the church. In chapter 15 of Acts, when the apostles met for the first council in Jerusalem, James pointed out this fact: "Simeon hath declared how God at the first did visit the Gentiles, to take out of them a people for his name. And to this agree the words of the prophets; as it is written, After this I will return, and will build again the tabernacle of David, which is fallen down; and I will build again the ruins thereof, and I will set it up: That the residue of men might seek after the Lord, and all the Gentiles, upon whom my name is called, saith the Lord, who doeth all these things. Known unto God are all his works from the beginning of the world" (Acts 15:14–18). This is what God is doing today. He is visiting the Gentiles to take out of them a people to His name. That is, God is calling out of the world those people who will trust Christ, and the Holy Spirit baptizes them into the body of believers, the church.

So when the apostles asked Jesus whether He would restore the kingdom "at this time," His answer was that this was not the subject for discussion at that time. Nor is it the subject for discussion today. There are a great many people who say to me, "Don't you think the Lord will be coming soon?" Well, now, I'll let you in on something that is confidential between you and me: I do believe that He is coming soon. However, I don't have any authority to tell you that He is coming soon, because I don't know. Our Lord said it is not for us to know the times or the seasons. That is not the important part for us.

I do believe in prophecy. However, I think one can overemphasize it. To be built up in the faith you need more than a prophetic study.

Then what is our business today? Notice again that the Lord did not rebuke them. Instead, He showed that He had something else in mind. There is something else for us to do. It is not for us to know the times nor the seasons—the Father has put those in His own power—but here is your commission:

> **But ye shall receive power, after that the Holy Ghost is come upon you: and ye shall be witnesses unto me both in Jerusalem, and in all Judaea, and in Samaria, and unto the uttermost part of the earth [Acts 1:8].**

This is the commission that still holds for today. This is not given only to a corporate body, to the church as a body; it is not a corporate commission. This is a very personal command to each believer—personally, privately. This was given to these men even before the Holy Spirit had come and formed the church. It is a direct command for you and for me today. It is our business to get the Word of God out to the world. We can't say that it is up to the church to send missionaries and to give out the Gospel, and then sit back and let others do it. The all-important question is whether you are getting out the Word of God. Have you gone to the ends of the earth as a witness to the Gospel? Or do you support a missionary or a radio program that does? Are you personally involved? Today there are a great many people who want to talk about the times and seasons of His coming, but they don't want to get involved in getting out the Word of God. But that is His commission—not only to the apostles—that is His commission to you and me. I am of the opinion that if the Lord should suddenly appear to you or to me right where we are at this moment, He would not talk about the time of His coming, but He would talk about getting out the Gospel. He wants people to be saved. This is our commission.

In order to get this Gospel out, we need power. That was His promise: "Ye shall receive power." And we need the leading of the Lord. Although it is our business today to get out the Word of God, there is no power in us, there is no power in the church, but there is power in the Holy Spirit. It is the Holy Spirit who moves through an individual or through the church or through a radio program. The question is whether we permit Him to do so. "Ye shall receive power, after that the Holy Ghost is come upon you."

"Ye shall be witnesses unto me." Our witness is to Christ. He is the center of attraction. "In Jerusalem," which applied to us means our hometown, there should be a witness to Christ. "All Judaea" is equivalent to our community; "Samaria" represents the other side of the tracks, the folk we don't associate with. Although we may not meet with these people socially, we are to take the Gospel to them. Of course we can't associate with everybody. We can select our friends as everyone else does. That is part of the freedom which we have. There are folk who wouldn't want to associate with us. There are lots of folk who wouldn't want me around; I would crimp their style. But we have both the privilege and the responsibility to get the Word of God out to folk whether or not we associate with them socially.

Finally, this witness to Christ is to go to the uttermost part of the earth. We never should lose sight of the fact that this is the Lord's intention. He has told us if we love Him to keep His commandments. His command is personal. We can't pass this off on the crowd, and say "The church is doing it; so I don't need to get involved." How much are you involved, friend? What is your witness to Christ?

ASCENSION AND PROMISE OF THE RETURN
OF JESUS

And when he had spoken these things, while they beheld, he was taken up; and a cloud received him out of their sight [Acts 1:9].

The ascension of the Lord Jesus Christ is an important and significant miracle in the ministry of the Lord. This is especially true for our space age when eyes are turned aloft and we are talking about travel in space. Space travel isn't really new. The Lord Jesus took off, and He didn't need a launching pad or a space suit or a missile.

There was a cloud to receive Him. What kind of a cloud was that? Was it a moisture cloud? No, this was the same *shekinah* glory cloud that had filled the tabernacle. In His high priestly prayer He had prayed: "And now, O Father, glorify thou me with thine own self with the glory which I had with thee before the world was" (John 17:5). When He was born into this world, He was wrapped in swaddling clothes. When He left this earth, He was wrapped in glory clouds. This is the way He returned to the Father's right hand.

While the apostles are watching all this, two angels appear to them. They look like men, and they have an important message.

> **And while they looked stedfastly toward heaven as he went up, behold, two men stood by them in white apparel;**
>
> **Which also said, Ye men of Galilee, why stand ye gazing up into heaven? this same Jesus, which is taken up from you into heaven, shall so come in like manner as ye have seen him go into heaven [Acts 1:10–11].**

It is the glorified Jesus who went up into heaven. This same Jesus, the glorified Jesus, will return in like manner and to the same place. Zechariah 14:4 tells us: "And his feet shall stand in that day upon the mount of Olives, which is before Jerusalem on the east, and the mount of Olives shall cleave in the midst thereof toward the east and toward the west, and there shall be a very great valley; and half of the mountain shall remove toward the north, and half of it toward the south." He took off at that place, and He will come back to that place.

WAITING FOR THE SPIRIT

> **Then returned they unto Jerusalem from the mount called Olivet, which is from Jerusalem a sabbath day's journey [Acts 1:12].**

"A sabbath day's journey," which was less than one mile, kept people pretty much in their location. That was why they would all camp very close to the temple during the feast days when they came to Jerusalem to worship. The Mount of Olives would probably be covered with people camping out, possibly several hundred thousand of them at the time of the feasts. Why? Because they needed to stay within a Sabbath day's journey of the temple.

> And when they were come in, they went up into an upper room, where abode both Peter, and James, and John, and Andrew, Philip, and Thomas, Bartholomew, and Matthew, James the son of Alphaeus, and Simon Zelotes, and Judas the brother of James.

> These all continued with one accord in prayer and supplication, with the women, and Mary the mother of Jesus, and with his brethren [Acts 1:13-14].

I rejoice that Mary, the mother of Jesus, was there. Her reputation has now been cleared. At this point it was obvious that Jesus was the Son of God, and virgin born, as she had claimed.

The attitude of the apostles and the other believers was that of oneness, of prayer, and of waiting.

There is no way that we can duplicate this period today. Remember that this is in a time period, a time capsule, between His ascension into heaven and the coming of the Holy Spirit. You and I do not live in that time period. It cannot be duplicated. We are not waiting for the coming of the Holy Spirit; He came over nineteen hundred years ago.

APPOINTMENT OF AN APOSTLE

> And in those days Peter stood up in the midst of the disciples, and said, (the number of names together were about an hundred and twenty,)

> Men and brethren, this scripture must needs have been fulfilled, which the Holy Ghost by the mouth of David

spake before concerning Judas, which was guide to them that took Jesus.

For he was numbered with us, and had obtained part of this ministry.

Now this man purchased a field with the reward of iniquity; and falling headlong, he burst asunder in the midst, and all his bowels gushed out [Acts 1:15–18].

Here is Simon Peter speaking up again. Note that this is *before* the Holy Spirit came at Pentecost. This man needs the filling of the Holy Spirit—and so do you and I.

He certainly gives a vivid picture of Judas, doesn't he?

If you are bothered by a seeming discrepancy here and with Matthew 27:5, the following quotation from *Unger's Bible Dictionary* by Merrill F. Unger (pp. 615–616) will be helpful to you.

NOTE.—Between these two passages (Matt. 27:5; Acts 1:16–25) there appears at first sight a discrepancy. In Matthew it is stated "He cast down the pieces of silver in the temple and departed, and went and hanged himself." In Acts (ch. 1) another account is given. There it is stated: (1) That instead of throwing the money into the temple he bought a field with it. (2) That instead of hanging himself, "falling headlong, he burst asunder in the midst, and all his bowels gushed out." (3) That for this reason, and not because the priests had bought it with the price of blood, the field was called "Aceldama." The fact would seem to be that Judas hanged himself, probably with his girdle, which either broke or became untied, and threw him heavily forward upon the jagged rocks below, thus inflicting the wound mentioned by Peter in the Acts. The apparent discrepancy in the two accounts as to the disposition of the money may be thus explained: "It was not lawful to take into the temple treasury, for the purchase of sacred things, money that had been unlawfully gained. In such case the Jewish law provided that the money was to be restored to the donor, and, if he insisted on giving it that he should be induced to spend it for something for the public weal. By a fiction of law the money was still considered to be Judas's, and to have been applied by him in the purchase of the well-known 'potter's field'" (Edersheim, *Life of Jesus*, ii, 575).

> **And it was known unto all the dwellers at Jerusalem; insomuch as that field is called in their proper tongue, Aceldama, that is to say, The field of blood.**

> **For it is written in the book of Psalms, Let his habitation be desolate, and let no man dwell therein: and his bishopric let another take [Acts 1:19–20].**

There is always a question about what happened here. Should Simon Peter have held this election to choose a man to take the place of Judas? I don't think so.

> **Wherefore of these men which have companied with us all the time that the Lord Jesus went in and out among us,**

> **Beginning from the baptism of John, unto that same day that he was taken up from us, must one be ordained to be a witness with us of his resurrection [Acts 1:21–22].**

I believe that the election to choose a successor to Judas Iscariot was conducted by Peter without the presence and guidance of the Holy Spirit. The Holy Spirit had not yet been given. Matthias was evidently a good man. He met the requirements of an apostle, which meant he must have seen the resurrected Christ, as that was a necessary requirement.

> **And they appointed two, Joseph called Barsabas, who was surnamed Justus, and Matthias.**

> **And they prayed, and said, Thou, Lord, which knowest the hearts of all men, shew whether of these two thou hast chosen,**

> That he may take part of this ministry and apostleship, from which Judas by transgression fell, that he might go to his own place.
>
> And they gave forth their lots; and the lot fell upon Matthias; and he was numbered with the eleven apostles [Acts 1:23–26].

I can't see that this was the leading of the Holy Spirit, nor that it was God's leading in the casting of lots. Is Matthias actually the one who took the place of Judas? I don't think so. I believe that in His own time, the Lord Jesus himself appointed one to take the place of Judas Iscariot. We don't hear another word about Matthias—nothing is recorded of his ministry. I think the Holy Spirit ignored Matthias. It is my conviction that the man the Lord chose was Paul. You may ask, "Do you have an authority for that statement?" Yes. Listen to Paul as he writes to the Galatian believers: "Paul, an apostle, (not of men, neither by man, but by Jesus Christ, and God the Father, who raised him from the dead;)" (Gal. 1:1). Paul is saying that he was chosen by God the Father and the Lord Jesus Christ. How did He do it? Through the Holy Spirit whom He had sent into the world. The ministry of Paul certainly justifies the fact that he was the one to take Judas' place. Of course I realize that the majority of good Bible commentators disagree with me, but I am just passing on to you my own conviction.

It is remarkable, and I want to mention again how Acts 1 brings the four Gospels to a focal point. Matthew concludes with the Resurrection, Mark with the Ascension, Luke with the promise of the Holy Spirit, and John with the promise of the Second Coming. Acts 1 brings all four records together and mentions each of them. The four Gospels funnel into Acts, and Acts is the bridge between the Gospels and the Epistles.

CHAPTER 2

THEME: The Day of Pentecost

We can divide this chapter into two sections. The coming of the Holy Spirit is recorded in verses 1–13. The first sermon in the church age, given by the apostle Peter, is recorded in verses 14–47.

COMING OF THE HOLY SPIRIT

And when the day of Pentecost was fully come, they were all with one accord in one place [Acts 2:1].

The words *fully come* could be translated "fulfilled." When the Day of Pentecost was being fulfilled, they were all together in one place.

Pentecost took place fifty days after the Feast of Firstfruits. You may remember in our study in Leviticus that we found that the Feast of Firstfruits speaks of the *resurrection* of Jesus Christ. Christ is the firstfruits—". . . Christ the firstfruits; afterward they that are Christ's at his coming" (1 Cor. 15:23).

The Passover speaks of the *death* of Jesus Christ, we learn from 1 Corinthians 5:7:". . . For even Christ our passover is sacrificed for us." Since the Passover has been fulfilled in the death of Christ, and the Feast of Firstfruits has been fulfilled in the resurrection of Christ, we believe that the Feast of Pentecost represents something—that is, it is the fulfillment of something. Its fulfillment is the birth of the church, the day the church came into existence.

When the Day of Pentecost "was being fulfilled," or "was fully come," means that this was the fulfillment of the meaning and the purpose for which it was given originally. On Pentecost there was to be a meal offering to the Lord, which was to be presented in two loaves of fine flour baked with leaven (Lev. 23). This was to depict the beginning and origin of the church. It spoke of the coming of the Holy Spirit in the very particular ministry of calling a people out of this world to

form the body of Christ, which is the church. Five minutes before the
Holy Spirit came on the Day of Pentecost there was no church. Five
minutes after the Holy Spirit came on the Day of Pentecost there was a
church. In other words, what Bethlehem was to the birth of Christ,
Jerusalem on the Day of Pentecost was to the coming of the Holy Spirit.
The Holy Spirit became incarnate. He began to baptize believers,
which means that the Holy Spirit identified them with Christ as His
body here on this earth. "For by one Spirit are we all baptized into one
body, whether we be Jews or Gentiles, whether we be bond or free; and
have been all made to drink into one Spirit" (1 Cor. 12:13).

The Holy Spirit began to perform a ministry on the Day of Pentecost. The Day of Pentecost was fulfilled on that day. When the Day of
Pentecost "was fully come" does not mean it was 12:00 noon or 7:00 in
the morning or 2:00 in the afternoon. It means that Pentecost, which
Israel had been celebrating for many generations, was fulfilled.

**And suddenly there came a sound from heaven as of a
rushing mighty wind, and it filled all the house where
they were sitting [Acts 2:2].**

Now I wish to call your attention to something that is very important.
When the Holy Spirit came, He was not visible. However, He made His
presence known in two ways. There was an appeal to two of the gates
through which all mankind gets his information: the ear-gate and the
eye-gate. We hear and we see. The Holy Spirit used both these gates.
Through the ear-gate they heard a sound from heaven *as of* a rushing
mighty wind. This sound filled the whole house where they were sitting.

Notice that it was not a wind; it was the sound *as of* a wind. It
wasn't like the sound of the wind blowing through the treetops. It
sounded like a tornado, and I believe that all of Jerusalem could hear it.
A friend of my daughter lives in Kansas and went through the experience of a tornado. It did not destroy their home but came within two
blocks of it. When she wrote about it to my daughter, she said, "The
first thing we noticed was a sound like a thousand freight trains coming into town." Friend, that was a rushing, mighty wind, and that was

the sound. It was that kind of sound that they heard on the Day of Pentecost.

And there appeared unto them cloven tongues like as of fire, and it sat upon each of them [Acts 2:3].

Again, I would call your attention to this. The tongues were *like as of* fire. It was not fire, but it looked like fire. This verse would be better translated, "There appeared unto them tongues parting asunder." That is, the tongues were like as a fire and it rested upon each of them. This was the appeal to the eye-gate. So on that Day of Pentecost, when the Holy Spirit came to the church, baptizing them into the body of Christ, there was an appeal to the ear and an appeal to the eye.

This is not to be confused with the baptism of fire. The baptism of fire is judgment which is yet to come. In the Book of Revelation we see the wrath of God revealed from heaven, fire from heaven. That is a baptism of fire. If men will not have the baptism of the Holy Spirit, then they must have the baptism of fire—judgment. The baptism of fire is for those who have rejected Jesus Christ.

I used to go to a prayer meeting which a wonderful preacher attended. I loved that dear brother, although his theology differed from mine in some points. He would always pray that fire would fall on us. And I always canceled out that prayer and said, "Lord, for goodness sake, don't let fire fall on us." Fire, you see, is judgment. Fire burns. That is yet to come. When the Holy Spirit came on the Day of Pentecost, they saw something that in appearance looked like fire.

And they were all filled with the Holy Ghost, and began to speak with other tongues, as the Spirit gave them utterance [Acts 2:4].

This verse says they were *filled* with the Holy Spirit. Someone may question the fact that I have been saying they were baptized with the Holy Spirit. Were they? Yes. The Lord Jesus told them they would be. "And, being assembled together with them, commanded them that they should not depart from Jerusalem, but wait for the promise of the

Father, which, saith he, ye have heard of me. For John truly baptized with water; but ye shall be baptized with the Holy Ghost not many days hence" (Acts 1:4-5). The very fact that they were filled with the Holy Spirit indicates that all the other ministries of the Holy Spirit to believers in this age had already been performed. They occurred in this order: First, they were regenerated. A man must be born again. "Jesus answered, Verily, verily, I say unto thee, Except a man be born of water and of the Spirit, he cannot enter into the kingdom of God" (John 3:5). Secondly, they were indwelt by the Spirit of God. "But ye are not in the flesh, but in the Spirit, if so be that the Spirit of God dwell in you. Now if any man have not the Spirit of Christ, he is none of his" (Rom. 8:9). Thirdly, they were sealed by the Holy Spirit into an eternal relationship with God. "In whom ye also trusted, after that ye heard the word of truth, the gospel of your salvation: in whom also after that ye believed, ye were sealed with that holy Spirit of promise, Which is the earnest of our inheritance until the redemption of the purchased possession, unto the praise of his glory" (Eph. 1:13-14). And again, "And grieve not the holy Spirit of God, whereby ye are sealed unto the day of redemption" (Eph. 4:30). It is possible to grieve the Spirit of God, but it is not possible to grieve Him away. He seals the believer unto the day of redemption. We are never told to ask for the sealing of the Holy Spirit. It is something which God does "after that ye believed," which is better translated "having believed." Faith in Jesus Christ gives us the sealing of the Holy Spirit unto the day of redemption.

Fourthly, they were baptized of the Holy Spirit. This was foretold by John the Baptist (Luke 3:16) and repeated by the Lord Jesus: "For John truly baptized with water; but ye shall be baptized with the Holy Ghost not many days hence" (Acts 1:5). The baptism took place, which placed them in the body of believers. It marked the beginning of the church. Ever since that day every believer in the Lord Jesus Christ is placed into the body of Christ by the baptism of the Holy Spirit. "For by one Spirit are we all baptized into one body, whether we be Jews or Gentiles, whether we be bond or free; and have been all made to drink into one Spirit" (1 Cor. 12:13).

Now when the filling of the Holy Spirit took place on the Day of Pentecost, it indicated that the other four ministries of the Holy Spirit had been accomplished. "And they were all filled with the Holy Ghost." The filling of the Spirit was for service. The *experience* of the Day of Pentecost came from the *filling* of the Holy Spirit (not the baptism of the Holy Spirit). It is still the same today. The filling of the Holy Spirit is for service. This is the only work of the Holy Spirit that we are to do anything about—we are commanded to be filled with the Holy Spirit: "And be not drunk with wine, wherein is excess; but be filled with the Spirit" (Eph. 5:18). Notice that before Pentecost the believers wanted this filling of the Spirit. "These all continued with one accord in prayer and supplication . . ." (Acts 1:14). What would their supplication be about? About the promise of the Lord Jesus that He would send His Holy Spirit to them.

The baptism of the Holy Spirit is not a command given to us. It is not an experience. It is an act of God whereby the believer in Jesus Christ is indwelt by the Spirit of God, sealed unto the day of redemption, and placed into the church, the body of Christ, by the baptism of the Spirit. The filling of the Spirit of God is the enablement for service. We are *commanded* to be filled with the Spirit.

After they were filled with the Holy Spirit, they "began to speak with other tongues, as the Spirit gave them utterance" (v. 4). These "other tongues" are not unknown tongues. There were many tongues spoken by Jews throughout the Roman Empire. These worshippers had come from the different areas of the Roman Empire for the Feast of Pentecost. Remember that all male Jews were required to come to Jerusalem for three of the feasts. They were in Jerusalem because of that, and many of them couldn't speak Hebrew.

That is not unusual. There are many Jews in our country today who cannot speak Hebrew. For years it was a dead language. In Israel today, Hebrew is being spoken again.

Now, my friend, the Day of Pentecost cannot be duplicated. It was a precise point in history. We cannot duplicate it any more than we can duplicate Bethlehem and the birth of Christ at Christmas.

Suppose the wise men had come back to Jerusalem again the next

year and had said, "Say, we're looking for the King of the Jews who is
born in Bethlehem." Suppose Herod would have said, "Weren't you
fellows here last year?" "Yes." "Well, did you find Him?" "Yes." "Well,
if He was born in Bethlehem last year, He isn't born there again this
year." "Oh, but we had such a wonderful experience here last year, we
thought we'd come back and do it all over again." Of course, Herod
would have answered, "Look, fellows, you can't duplicate that. He
was born in Bethlehem only once."

Just so, friend, you cannot duplicate Pentecost. The Holy Spirit
came on the Day of Pentecost. You don't have to beg Him to come or
urge Him to come. He is here. The Spirit of God is in the world today.
Jesus told us what He would do after He came: "He shall glorify me: for
he shall receive of mine, and shall shew it unto you" (John 16:14). We
know He is here when He takes the things of Christ and shows them to
us. And when we are talking about the things of Christ, the Spirit of
God has something that He can work with.

"As the Spirit gave them utterance." These apostles were from Galilee. They couldn't speak all these other languages. But they are speaking them now. The Spirit gave them utterance.

> **And there were dwelling at Jerusalem Jews, devout men,
> out of every nation under heaven [Acts 2:5].**

They had come from everywhere because of the Feast of Pentecost.
This was their reason for being in Jerusalem.

> **Now when this was noised abroad, the multitude came
> together, and were confounded, because that every man
> heard them speak in his own language [Acts 2:6].**

A better translation of "when this was noised abroad" is "when this
sound having taken place." Because of the sound as of a mighty rushing wind, a multitude came together. I shall never forget here in Pasadena, where I live, the first time we heard a jet plane break the sound
barrier. We were all out in our front yards wanting to know where the

sound had come from. We had never heard anything like it before. The sound the people of Jerusalem heard had never been heard before; so they came rushing toward it—which may have been to the temple area. Probably all 120 believers were there (Acts 1:15).

The people who rushed there were confounded because every man *heard*—in the Greek the imperfect tense is used, so that it should read, "every man was hearing"—them speak in his own dialect. It was not only that the language of their country was spoken, but each man heard his own dialect as it was spoken in his area of the country.

These men were not talking gibberish. They were not talking in unknown tongues. These men were speaking the dialects of the people in the multitude.

Now there is another aspect which I must mention. Some Bible scholars believe that what is meant here is that the apostles were not speaking in other languages at all, but were speaking in their own Galilean dialect, and the miracle was in the *hearing* because it says that every man *heard* them speak in his own dialect. Was the miracle that broke down the language barrier in the speaking or in the hearing?

> **And they were all amazed and marvelled, saying one to another, Behold, are not all these which speak Galilaeans?**
>
> **And how hear we every man in our own tongue, wherein we were born?**
>
> **Parthians, and Medes, and Elamites, and the dwellers in Mesopotamia, and in Judaea, and Cappadocia, in Pontus, and Asia,**
>
> **Phrygia, and Pamphylia, in Egypt, and in the parts of Libya about Cyrene, and strangers of Rome, Jews and proselytes,**
>
> **Cretes and Arabians, we do hear them speak in our tongues the wonderful works of God [Acts 2:7–11].**

Here were people from three continents. Certainly they were of diverse languages and dialects. They each heard these Galileans speak in an understandable dialect. May I say, these were not unknown tongues. They were languages that were understood.

And they were all amazed, and were in doubt, saying one to another, What meaneth this? [Acts 2:12].

They were amazed—*perplexed* would be a better word. They didn't understand what was taking place.

Others mocking said, These men are full of new wine [Acts 2:13].

The literal translation is *sweet wine,* and I understand that is a little more intoxicating. They thought these men were drunk.

Remember that Paul writes: "And be not drunk with wine, wherein is excess; but be filled with the Spirit" (Eph. 5:18). Have you noticed that a drunk man seems to have more power? He certainly is more talkative. Perhaps many of us today need the filling of the Spirit to make us talkative—not to speak in an unknown tongue, but power to speak the Gospel to others. That is the kind of tongues movement we need today. And by the way, we need a tongues movement of giving the Gospel in the language that the man can understand. That is all important.

What a day Pentecost was! It was the day the Holy Spirit came to call out a body of believers to form the church. The day before Pentecost there was no church. The day after Pentecost there was a church. Just as the Feast of Pentecost in the Old Testament followed fifty days after the Feast of the Firstfruits, so fifty days after the Lord Jesus arose from the dead, the Holy Spirit came to call out a body of believers.

Now Simon Peter is going to stand up and answer the mocking taunt that they are full of new wine.

FIRST SERMON IN THE CHURCH AGE, DELIVERED BY PETER

But Peter, standing up with the eleven, lifted up his voice, and said unto them, Ye men of Judaea, and all ye

that dwell at Jerusalem, be this known unto you, and
hearken to my words:

For these are not drunken, as ye suppose, seeing it is but
the third hour of the day [Acts 2:14–15].

Now I think that we need to recognize who the congregation was.
These were men of Judea and all that dwell at Jerusalem. In that day
Jerusalem was entirely a Jewish city. Pilate and his people had their
headquarters in Caesarea, not in Jerusalem. This early church was 100
percent Jewish. It was made up of Israelites. We need to recognize that.
The church began in Jerusalem, then moved out to Judea, than Samaria, and then to the uttermost parts of the earth. This has been the
movement of the church from that day to this. In the Old Testament it
was to Jerusalem that the world was to come for worship. Now they are
commanded to leave Jerusalem and to take this message to the ends of
the earth.

Peter replies to their mockery and ridicule by saying, "This could
not be drunkenness, because look at the time of day it is!" This was not
an hour when people in that day were drunk. He is talking to the
cynic.

Now Peter quotes to them from their own Scripture.

But this is that which was spoken by the prophet Joel
[Acts 2:16].

He uses this prophecy as an answer to the cynical, the unbeliever, the
mocker. This is his purpose for quoting it. He says, "That is that,"
which is, this is similar to or this is like that. He does not say that this
is the fulfillment of that which was spoken by the prophet Joel. He is
saying, "Why do you think this is something odd or something
strange? We have prophecy that says these things are going to come to
pass." Peter goes on to quote the prophecy from Joel. I'm glad Simon
Peter quoted as much as he did because he makes it obvious that he
was not attempting to say this was fulfilled. Now what is it that is to
come?

> And it shall come to pass in the last days, saith God, I
> will pour out of my Spirit upon all flesh: and your sons
> and your daughters shall prophesy, and your young men
> shall see visions, and your old men shall dream
> dreams:
>
> And on my servants and on my handmaidens I will
> pour out in those days of my Spirit; and they shall
> prophesy:
>
> And I will shew wonders in heaven above, and signs in
> the earth beneath; blood, and fire, and vapour of smoke:
>
> The sun shall be turned into darkness, and the moon
> into blood, before that great and notable day of the Lord
> come:
>
> And it shall come to pass, that whosoever shall call on
> the name of the Lord shall be saved [Acts 2:17–21].

I don't think that anyone would claim that on the Day of Pentecost the moon was turned to blood or that the sun was turned to darkness. When Christ was crucified, there was darkness for three hours, but not on the Day of Pentecost. Nor were there wonders of heaven above and signs in the earth beneath. Nor was there blood and fire and a vapor of smoke. Simon Peter quotes this passage to these mockers to show them that the pouring out of the Spirit of God should not be strange to them. Joel had predicted it, and it is going to come to pass.

My friend, Joel 2:28–32 has not been fulfilled to this day. If we turn back to the Book of Joel, we will find that he had a great deal to say about the Day of the Lord. The Day of the Lord will begin with the Great Tribulation Period. It will go on through the Millennium. In three chapters of the Book of Joel the Day of the Lord is mentioned five times. Joel talks about the fact that it is a time of war, a time of judgment upon the earth. That has not yet been fulfilled. It was not fulfilled on the Day of Pentecost.

If we could only see that all Simon Peter is saying in his introduction is, "Now look, this is not strange or contrary. The day is coming when this will be fulfilled. And today we are seeing something similar to it." Now after his introduction, he will move on to his text. Remember he is speaking to men who knew the Old Testament. Don't try to read nineteen hundred years of church history into this. This is just the beginning of the church on the Day of Pentecost. This is the inception of the church. Obviously he is speaking to the Jews—"Ye men of Israel." He doesn't say, "Ye men of Southern California." He is talking to Israelites. Now he is getting down to the nitty gritty. Now he is getting to his subject.

> **Ye men of Israel, hear these words; Jesus of Nazareth, a man approved of God among you by miracles and wonders and signs, which God did by him in the midst of you, as ye yourselves also know [Acts 2:22].**

Now I personally think that miracles and wonders and signs were all different. I believe that miracles were performed for one purpose, wonders for another purpose, and signs for another purpose. Jesus did certain things that were to be signs. Some miracles of healing were performed to get the attention of His hearers. These were the three areas in which our Lord moved.

> **Him, being delivered by the determinate counsel and foreknowledge of God, ye have taken, and by wicked hands have crucified and slain:**

> **Whom God hath raised up, having loosed the pains of death: because it was not possible that he should be holden of it [Acts 2:23–24].**

Peter is saying that what has happened was not contrary to God's program. This is not something that took God by surprise. However, he makes it clear that this does not release men from their responsibility. Who is responsible for the crucifixion of Christ? The religious rulers were the ones who began the movement. I would say that they were largely to blame. They moved upon the multitude so that they produced mob action. They also maneuvered the Roman government to execute Him. Remember, friend, He was crucified on a Roman cross. Peter is pointing his finger at his fellow Israelites.

But there is no use in our arguing about who was responsible for His death back at that time. I'll tell you who is responsible for His death. You are responsible, and I am responsible. It was for my sins and for your sins that He died. Listen to the words of Jesus: "Therefore doth my Father love me, because I lay down my life, that I might take it again. No man taketh it from me, but I lay it down of myself. I have power to lay it down, and I have power to take it again. This command- ment have I received of my Father" (John 10:17–18).

Peter is speaking to men who were directly involved in the plot of the Crucifixion, and he says, "Ye have taken, and by wicked hands have crucified and slain."

However, that is not the most important part of his message. He goes on, "Whom God hath raised up, having loosed the pains of death." He preaches the resurrection of Jesus Christ. This is the first sermon ever preached in the church age. This is the beginning. This is the Day of Pentecost. What is his theme? It is not the prophecy of Joel, my friend. It is the resurrection of the Lord Jesus Christ. Let's not try to change his subject! Now he is going to quote his text. He quotes from Psalm 16:8–10. I am glad he did that because this helps me to under- stand Psalm 16.

> **For David speaketh concerning him, I foresaw the Lord always before my face, for he is on my right hand, that I should not be moved:**
>
> **Therefore did my heart rejoice, and my tongue was glad; moreover also my flesh shall rest in hope:**
>
> **Because thou wilt not leave my soul in hell, neither wilt thou suffer thine Holy One to see corruption [Acts 2:25–27].**

The word *hell* should be "sheol." In that day it was sheol.

**Thou hast made known to me the ways of life; thou shalt
make me full of joy with thy countenance [Acts 2:28].**

In Psalm 16 David is talking about the resurrection of Christ. This has
now been fulfilled. The interpretation of this psalm is given by Simon
Peter, who is filled with the Holy Spirit.

**Men and brethren, let me freely speak unto you of the
patriarch David, that he is both dead and buried, and
his sepulchre is with us unto this day [Acts 2:29].**

Apparently Peter was standing in the temple area. He could point his
finger to the sepulchre of David. I have stood in that temple area, and I
could point my finger up to the top of Mount Zion where David is
buried. He is saying, "It is obvious that David wasn't speaking about
himself because his bones are right up there on the top of the hill. His
grave is there; his body did undergo corruption. He is not speaking of
himself but of Someone whom you and I know, Someone who did not
see corruption but was raised from the dead."

**Therefore being a prophet, and knowing that God had
sworn with an oath to him, that of the fruit of his loins,
according to the flesh, he would raise up Christ to sit on
his throne;**

**He seeing this before spake of the resurrection of Christ,
that his soul was not left in hell, neither his flesh did see
corruption [Acts 2:30–31].**

This is what David was talking about in Psalm 16. He was speaking of
the resurrection of Jesus Christ. You may say, "But I read Psalm 16,
and it doesn't say that Jesus Christ will rise from the dead." My friend,
here in Acts 2 we have the Holy Spirit's interpretation of this psalm.
Now we can go back and read the psalm, knowing that it refers to the
resurrection of the Lord Jesus.

What is Simon Peter talking about? His sermon is about the resur-

rection of Jesus Christ. The first sermon ever preached in the church
age was an Easter sermon. And every sermon in the early church was
an Easter sermon.

> **This Jesus hath God raised up, whereof we all are wit-
> nesses [Acts 2:32].**

Now Peter is saying to the crowd there that day, "This that you have
seen—that is, the miracle of hearing their own languages spoken by
Galileans—has taken place because Jesus was raised from the dead."

> **Therefore being by the right hand of God exalted, and
> having received of the Father the promise of the Holy
> Ghost, he hath shed forth this, which ye now see and
> hear.**

> **For David is not ascended into the heavens: but he saith
> himself, The LORD said unto my Lord, Sit thou on my
> right hand,**

> **Until I make thy foes thy footstool [Acts 2:33–35].**

Old Testament saints didn't go to heaven. If any of them had been up in
heaven, David would have been there. David did not ascend into
heaven. You see, the Old Testament saints are going to be raised to live
down on this earth someday. It is the church that will be taken to the
New Jerusalem. It is said of the believers today when they die that they
are absent from the body and present with the Lord (2 Cor. 5:8).

Now he quotes Psalm 110:1. He is showing them that Jesus is up
yonder at the right hand of God. He will be there until He comes back
to establish His kingdom. But while He is at the right hand of God, He
is still working in the world.

> **Therefore let all the house of Israel know assuredly, that
> God hath made that same Jesus, whom ye have cruci-
> fied, both Lord and Christ [Acts 2:36].**

He is preaching the resurrection of Jesus Christ—that Christ died for their sins, but He rose again.

> **Now when they heard this, they were pricked in their heart, and said unto Peter and to the rest of the apostles, Men and brethren, what shall we do? [Acts 2:37].**

The message of Simon Peter brought conviction to them.

> **Then Peter said unto them, Repent, and be baptized every one of you in the name of Jesus Christ for the remission of sins, and ye shall receive the gift of the Holy Ghost [Acts 2:38].**

This is for a people who had the Word of God, who had heard the message, who knew the prophecies. They had been going along in one direction, which was away from God, even though they had a God-given religion. They are told to repent. They are to turn around and come God's way.

Peter says to them, "Repent, and be baptized." Water baptism would be the evidence that they had repented, that they had come to Christ and had put their trust in Him.

Peter says to them, "Be baptized . . . in the name of Jesus Christ for the remission of sins. This will be an evidence that you have trusted Him for the remission of your sins—rather than bringing a sacrifice to be offered in the temple." You see, their baptism would be a testimony to the fact that Christ is the Lamb of God who takes away the sin of the world.

"And ye shall receive the gift of the Holy Ghost." Anyone who believes, who puts his trust in Jesus Christ, will receive the gift of the Holy Spirit.

> **For the promise is unto you, and to your children, and to all that are afar off, even as many as the Lord our God shall call [Acts 2:39].**

Nineteen hundred years ago you and I were "afar off." He is talking about us here.

> **And with many other words did he testify and exhort, saying, Save yourselves from this untoward generation [Acts 2:40].**

In other words, "Get away from this religion. Turn to Christ."

> **Then they that gladly received his word were baptized: and the same day there were added unto them about three thousand souls [Acts 2:41].**

This is not some preacher's count. These were genuinely born-again believers. Here is one place where the figure on the number of converts is absolutely accurate.

THE CHURCH WHICH HAS COME INTO EXISTENCE

> **And they continued stedfastly in the apostles' doctrine and fellowship, and in breaking of bread, and in prayers [Acts 2:42].**

I have a little booklet called the *Spiritual Fingerprints of the Visible Church*. How can you identify a real church? Notice the four marks of identification. First, *They continued stedfastly in the apostles' doctrine*. The mark of a church is not the height of the steeple nor the sound of the bell. It is not whether the pulpit is stationed in the middle or the chancel is divided. The important issue is whether or not they hold to the apostles' doctrine. Correct doctrine was one of the fingerprints of the visible church. Secondly, *fellowship*. They were sharing the things of Christ. The third, *breaking of bread*. Breaking of bread is more than just going through the ritual of the Lord's Supper. It means being brought into a fellowship and a relationship with Christ. The fourth, *prayers*. I'm afraid in the average church today it is a little fingerprint. That is, prayer is the evident weakness of the church. Actually, the greatest asset of any church is prayer.

> **And fear came upon every soul: and many wonders and signs were done by the apostles [Acts 2:43].**

It was the apostles who had the sign gifts.

> **And all that believed were together, and had all things common;**
>
> **And sold their possessions and goods, and parted them to all men, as every man had need.**
>
> **And they, continuing daily with one accord in the temple, and breaking bread from house to house, did eat their meat with gladness and singleness of heart,**
>
> **Praising God, and having favour with all the people. And the Lord added to the church daily such as should be saved [Acts 2:44–47].**

Never has the church been as spiritually strong as it was at that time. This type of living would never work today because we have too many carnal Christians. And, notice, it was the Lord who did the adding to the church.

CHAPTER 3

THEME: First miracle of the church; Peter's second sermon

We are still in the first division of the Book of Acts which shows the Lord Jesus Christ at work by the Holy Spirit through the apostles in Jerusalem. We have seen the birthday of the church on the Day of Pentecost, a day which can never be repeated. There was a church because the Holy Spirit had become incarnate in believers. He was indwelling the believers, and He filled them with His love, power, and blessing for service.

Just as you and I cannot repeat Bethlehem, neither can we repeat Pentecost. But we do need the power of the Holy Spirit today. Thank God, He is in the world, convicting the world, restraining evil in the world. We don't have to seek Him; He is indwelling all believers in the Lord Jesus Christ.

In this third chapter we will find the healing of the lame man, verses 1–11. The appealing and revealing address of Peter is in verses 12–26. The result was five thousand men who believed!

HEALING OF LAME MAN

Now Peter and John went up together into the temple at the hour of prayer, being the ninth hour [Acts 3:1].

This apparently was the time of the evening sacrifice when a priest went in to offer incense with his prayers. We find in the first chapter of Luke that this was the service Zacharias was performing when he went to minister before the golden altar and the angel appeared to him. That golden altar, the altar of incense, speaks of prayer. This was the time of prayer. There would be a great company in the temple area praying at this time.

> And a certain man lame from his mother's womb was
> carried, whom they laid daily at the gate of the temple
> which is called Beautiful, to ask alms of them that en-
> tered into the temple [Acts 3:2].

This man had been born lame. He was brought every day and put there
at the gate of the temple. What a contrast he was to the gate which is
called Beautiful. Here was a beautiful gate, and here was a man who
was married. Man can make beautiful things, but man cannot improve
himself. Of course, man can do some trimming on the outside. He can
cut his hair, have his fingernails manicured, take a bath now and then,
but man can never change that old nature which he has. This is the
contrast we have here—a beautiful gate of the temple and a man lame
from his mother's womb.

He was there to beg for alms. This was the way he lived, of course.

> Who seeing Peter and John about to go into the temple
> asked an alms [Acts 3:3].

This shows us that after the Day of Pentecost, Peter and John still went
up to the temple to pray. All the believers there in Jerusalem were Isra-
lites or proselytes, and they continued to go to the temple to pray. The
poor beggar saw Peter and John, and he hoped that they would be able
to give him something.

> And Peter, fastening his eyes upon him with John, said,
> Look on us.

> And he gave heed unto them, expecting to receive some-
> thing of them [Acts 3:4–5].

When these two men gave him this much attention, the beggar looked
at them with the certainty that they would give him something.

> Then Peter said, Silver and gold have I none; but such as
> I have give I thee: In the name of Jesus Christ of Naza-
> reth rise up and walk [Acts 3:6].

An incident is told of one of the early saints of the church in Rome who walked in on the pope as he was counting money. Realizing that he had walked in on something which was private, he started to walk out. The pope said to him, "No longer can the church say 'Silver and gold have I none.'" As the saintly man continued walking out, he said, "Neither can the church say to the impotent man, 'Rise up and walk.'"

Today the organized church has wealth. I suppose that if one could put together all the holdings of all the churches, all groups, denominations, and non-denominations across the country, we would find the church wealthier than any other organization. I think it is wealthier than the Standard Oil Company. Yet the church today lacks power.

Now notice what Peter does.

> **And he took him by the right hand, and lifted him up: and immediately his feet and ankle bones received strength [Acts 3:7].**

Remember that Dr. Luke wrote this book. You will notice that when Dr. Luke records a miracle, he gives a great many details which we don't find in some other books. He tells specifically what happened. The weakness had been in the feet and ankle bones of this man.

> **And he leaping up stood, and walked, and entered with them into the temple, walking, and leaping, and praising God [Acts 3:8].**

Friend, don't miss this word *leaping*. It occurs twice in this verse.

This is a very interesting chapter. We will find that Peter is going to offer the kingdom to the nation again because at this time the church is 100 percent Israelite. There are no Gentiles from the outside. The church began with the Jews in Jerusalem. Later, it will go to the ends of the earth. But this, now, is the Jerusalem period.

Don't try to tell me this is another dispensation. We have hyperdispensationalists today who call this another dispensation. It is not different at all. But it is a period of transition. The Lord had said they were to begin by going out to the ends of the earth.

Now the kingdom is being offered to Israel again. This will be the final opportunity. What will be some of the identifying marks of the kingdom? Well, one is that the lame shall leap! "Then shall the lame man leap as an hart, and the tongue of the dumb sing: for in the wilderness shall waters break out, and streams in the desert" (Isa. 35:6).

Every instructed Israelite going up to the temple that day marveled at this lame man leaping. They knew this could actually be the beginning of the kingdom. The Messiah had been crucified, raised from the dead, ascended to heaven, and seated at God's right hand. If they would receive Him, He would come again.

And all the people saw him walking and praising God:

And they knew that it was he which sat for alms at the Beautiful gate of the temple: and they were filled with wonder and amazement at that which had happened unto him [Acts 3:9–10].

They saw him. They recognized the man. They caught the significance of this miracle. I'm afraid there are a great many today who haven't caught the significance of this record which Dr. Luke has given us.

And as the lame man which was healed held Peter and John, all the people ran together unto them in the porch that is called Solomon's, greatly wondering [Acts 3:11].

Is this to be the beginning of the kingdom? Great things had happened in Jerusalem during the past few weeks. They had witnessed the crucifixion of Jesus, His resurrection, His ascension, and the Day of Pentecost. They are amazed. What is really taking place?

THE APPEALING AND REVEALING ADDRESS
OF PETER

And when Peter saw it, he answered unto the people, Ye men of Israel, why marvel ye at this? or why look ye so

earnestly on us, as though by our own power or holiness
we had made this man to walk? [Acts 3:12].

He doesn't say, "Ye men of the United States." He is talking to the men
of Israel. This is the Jerusalem period, friend. This is the transition
period. The church has not yet moved out to other areas. No one in
Rome has heard yet. No one in America has heard. No one in England
has heard. This is in Jerusalem.

May I say something kindly? Folk reading the Bible should bring to
it the same common sense they use in reading other books. This is
God's Book. But it is not some "way out yonder" type of book. It deals
with us right where we are, and it communicates so we can understand it.

Peter is very careful to tell them that this miracle was not done in
his own power. He is going to direct this Jewish audience back to the
Old Testament. He is going to tell them that if they will turn to God,
these prophecies can be fulfilled.

Listen to some of the prophecies which these Jewish people knew.
"And I will pour upon the house of David, and upon the inhabitants of
Jerusalem, the spirit of grace and of supplications: and they shall look
upon me whom they have pierced, and they shall mourn for him, as
one mourneth for his only son, and shall be in bitterness for him, as
one that is in bitterness for his firstborn" (Zech. 12:10). This would be
fulfilled if they would turn to Him. It was not fulfilled because the
nation did not accept the Lord Jesus at that time. They did not repent
and turn to Him. Peter will invite them to turn to the Lord Jesus. They
will refuse. The time is still to come when this will be fulfilled. Also
Ezekiel spoke of the kingdom: "And I will put my spirit within you,
and cause you to walk in my statutes, and ye shall keep my judgments,
and do them. And ye shall dwell in the land that I gave to your fathers;
and ye shall be my people, and I will be your God" (Ezek. 36:27–28).
Notice the twelfth chapter of Isaiah, a remarkable chapter—only six
verses—that speaks of the worship during the time of the kingdom:
"And in that day thou shalt say, O LORD, I will praise thee: though thou
wast angry with me, thine anger is turned away, and thou comfortedst
me, Behold, God is my salvation; I will trust, and not be afraid: for the

LORD JEHOVAH is my strength and my song; he also is become my
salvation" (Isa. 12:1–2). Also, as we have mentioned, Isaiah 35:6 told
of the lame man leaping as an hart. "And the ransomed of the LORD
shall return, and come to Zion with songs and everlasting joy upon
their heads: they shall obtain joy and gladness, and sorrow and sigh-
ing shall flee away" (Isa. 35:10). They should have seen that this lame
man was a miniature, a picture of the whole nation. If they would but
turn to God, all these promises would be fulfilled.

> **The God of Abraham, and of Isaac, and of Jacob, the
> God of our fathers, hath glorified his Son Jesus; whom
> ye delivered up, and denied him in the presence of Pi-
> late, when he was determined to let him go.**

> **But ye denied the Holy One and the Just, and desired a
> murderer to be granted unto you;**

> **And killed the Prince of life, whom God hath raised
> from the dead; whereof we are witnesses [Acts 3:13–15].**

Here he goes again. Simon Peter will never preach a sermon without
the mention of the Resurrection. Paul won't either. Unfortunately, today there are many sermons preached without a mention of the Resurrection.

> **And his name through faith in his name hath made this
> man strong, whom ye see and know: yea, the faith
> which is by him hath given him this perfect soundness
> in the presence of you all [Acts 3:16].**

In essence Peter is saying, "Don't you see that man leaping there? That
is what they will do in the kingdom. The question is whether or not
you want the Messiah to come back. Do you want to receive Him?"

> **And now, brethren, I wot that through ignorance ye did
> it, as did also your rulers.**

**But those things, which God before had shewed by the
mouth of all his prophets, that Christ should suffer, he
hath so fulfilled [Acts 3:17–18].**

Their past deeds call for a course of action. That action is repentance
and conversion. This was not a new message to them. "I, even I, am he
that blotteth out thy transgressions for mine own sake, and will not
remember thy sins" (Isa. 43:25). Listen to Peter's message:

**Repent ye therefore, and be converted, that your sins
may be blotted out, when the times of refreshing shall
come from the presence of the Lord;**

**And he shall send Jesus Christ, which before was
preached unto you [Acts 3:19–20].**

If they had accepted Jesus, would He have returned to the earth? The
answer, of course, is yes. Peter says He would have. Then what would
have been God's program after that? I'll tell you something today that
will be a secret just between you and me: I don't know what would
have happened. Does that come as a surprise to you? Well, I have news
for you. No one else knows either—no one except God. We can ask
innumerable "if" questions to which there are no answers. All I know
is that the nation did not accept Jesus Christ. That is the only answer I
know to the "if" question. Any other answer would be only the wildest
speculation.

**And he shall send Jesus Christ, which before was
preached unto you:**

**Whom the heaven must receive until the times of restitu-
tion of all things, which God hath spoken by the mouth
of all his holy prophets since the world began [Acts
3:20–21].**

Some folk use this verse to bolster their belief that eventually everything and every person will be saved. "The restitution of all things" is

the phrase they use. Exactly what are the "all things" which are to be the subject of restitution? In Philippians 3:8 when Paul said, ". . . I count all things but loss . . ." did he mean all things in God's universe? Obviously not. So here, the "all things" are limited by what follows. "The times of restitution of all things, which God hath spoken by the mouth of all his holy prophets since the world began." The prophets had spoken of the restoration of Israel. Nowhere is there a prophecy of the conversion and restoration of the wicked dead.

> **For Moses truly said unto the fathers, A prophet shall the Lord your God raise up unto you of your brethren, like unto me; him shall ye hear in all things whatsoever he shall say unto you.**
>
> **And it shall come to pass, that every soul, which will not hear that prophet, shall be destroyed from among the people [Acts 3:22-23].**

The nation of Israel was on the verge of a great judgment. In A.D. 70 Titus, the Roman general, came with his army and destroyed the city. It is estimated that over a million people perished, and the rest were sold into slavery throughout the Roman Empire. Judgment did come upon these people.

> **Yea, and all the prophets from Samuel and those that follow after, as many as have spoken, have likewise foretold of these days.**
>
> **Ye are the children of the prophets, and of the covenant which God made with our fathers, saying unto Abraham, And in thy seed shall all the kindreds of the earth be blessed.**
>
> **Unto you first God, having raised up his Son Jesus, sent him to bless you, in turning away every one of you from his iniquities [Acts 3:24-26].**

This is a transition period. They were given their final chance to accept the Messiah. Because they turned down their opportunity to accept the Messiah, later on Paul will come on the scene as the apostle to the Gentiles. What might have happened if they had turned to God is merely speculation. They did not turn to Him. God is never surprised by what man does, and He still works things out according to His plan and purpose.

CHAPTER 4

THEME: First persecution of the church; power of the
Holy Spirit

This chapter shows the result of Peter's second sermon. Five thousand people were saved. Then the apostles were arrested and put into prison. This was at the instigation of the Sadducees, and the reason for it was the preaching of the resurrection of Jesus Christ.

FIRST PERSECUTION OF THE CHURCH

And as they spake unto the people, the priests, and the captain of the temple, and the Sadducees, came upon them,

Being grieved that they taught the people, and preached through Jesus the resurrection from the dead [Acts 4:1–2].

I want to call your attention to something that is quite startling and interesting to see. Who was it that led in the persecution of the Lord Jesus and finally had Him arrested and put to death? It was the religious rulers, the Pharisees. They were the enemies of Christ as He walked here on earth. Apparently quite a few of the Pharisees were saved. We know that Nicodemus was. Joseph of Arimathea may have been a Pharisee. We know that Saul of Tarsus was one. Apparently there were many others of the Pharisees who were brought to a saving knowledge of the Lord Jesus Christ. After they had gotten rid of Him, their enmity and their spite were over.

Now the Sadducees, who do not believe in resurrection, become the great enemies when the church comes into existence because the apostles are preaching the resurrection of Jesus Christ.

Let me give you an illustration of this. I have never engaged in any movement or reformation to try to straighten up any of the places where I preached. I never felt that was my job. I was a pastor in downtown Los Angeles for many years. In that town we had movie stars who had their day, but then the stardom disappeared and they became burned-out cinders. Often they would go into some kind of reformation work after their star had gone out. Maybe that was some type of reaction, I don't know. Such a woman called and asked me to serve on a committee that was trying to clean up downtown Los Angeles. I agreed it needed cleaning up, but I told her that I could not serve on the committee. She was amazed. "Aren't you a minister?" she asked. "Aren't you interested in cleaning up Los Angeles?" I answered, "I will not serve on your committee because I don't think you are going about it in the right way." Then I told her what the late Dr. Bob Shuler had told me years ago. He said, "We are called to fish in the fish pond, not to clean up the fish pond." This old world is a place to fish. Jesus said He would make us fishers of men, and the world is the place to fish. We are not called upon to clean up the fish pond. We need to catch the fish and get the fish cleaned up.

I have found that the biggest enemies of the preaching of the Gospel are not the liquor folk. The gangsters have never bothered me. Do you know where I had my trouble as a preacher? It was with the so-called religious leaders, the liberals, those who claimed to be born again. They actually became enemies of the preaching of the Gospel. It was amazing to me to find out how many of them wanted to destroy my radio ministry. They were our worst antagonists. It was not the gangsters, not the unsaved folk, but these religious leaders. They are the Sadducees of today. They are the ones who deny the supernatural. They deny the Word of God either by their lips or by their lives. That is important to see.

The Sadducees of that day and the "Sadducees" of our day try to make trouble for anyone who preaches the Resurrection. You can preach Jesus, friend. You can make Him a nice, sweet individual, a sort of Casper Milquetoast, and you will not be in trouble. But you are in trouble if you preach Him as the mighty Savior who came down to this earth, denounced sin, died on the cross for the sins of men, and then rose again in mighty power. That is the hated message. When the apostles preached it, the Sadducees arrested them and brought them in to the Sanhedrin.

> **And they laid hands on them, and put them in hold unto the next day: for it was now eventide.**
>
> **Howbeit many of them which heard the word believed; and the number of the men was about five thousand [Acts 4:3–4].**

All this was happening at Solomon's porch following the sermon which Peter had delivered. If there were five thousand men who believed, how many women and children do you suppose might have believed? This was a whole multitude that turned to Christ.

I have always been reluctant to criticize Simon Peter. You can't help but love the man. He was mightily used of God. This is not an evangelistic meeting where figures are turned in rather carelessly. These are genuine converts. There is nothing like this on record from that day to the present day, and I don't believe it will be exceeded as long as the church is in the world.

> **And it came to pass on the morrow, that their rulers, and elders, and scribes,**
>
> **And Annas the high priest, and Caiaphas, and John, and Alexander, and as many as were of the kindred of the high priest, were gathered together at Jerusalem [Acts 4:5–6].**

We have met this crowd before. These are the sneaky fellows, Annas and Caiaphas, in the background. These are the two men who condemned Jesus to die.

> **And when they had set them in the midst, they asked, By what power, or by what name, have ye done this? [Acts 4:7].**

Peter and John are brought before the Sanhedrin. The lame man had been healed, and Peter had preached his second sermon. The Sanhedrin demands to know by what power and by what name they do these things.

Then Peter, filled with the Holy Ghost, said unto them, Ye rulers of the people, and elders of Israel [Acts 4:8].

Notice that Peter is *filled* with the Holy Spirit. He wasn't baptized by the Holy Spirit at this time—that had already been accomplished. However he was filled with the Holy Spirit. You and I also need the filling of the Holy Spirit. That is something we should seek after; it is something we should devoutly want. Don't tarry and wait for the baptism of the Spirit. They had to tarry and wait until the Day of Pentecost when they were all baptized into one body, but today if you will turn to Jesus Christ, you will be baptized with the Holy Spirit and placed into the body of believers at the very moment you are regenerated.

If we this day be examined of the good deed done to the impotent man, by what means he is made whole;

Be it known unto you all, and to all the people of Israel, that by the name of Jesus Christ of Nazareth, whom ye crucified, whom God raised from the dead, even by him doth this man stand here before you whole [Acts 4:9–10].

Peter does a good job of speaking to these men. Up to this time, every time Peter opened his mouth, he put his foot in it. But this time, I tell you, he has his ". . . feet shod with the preparation of the gospel of peace" (Eph. 6:15). He is filled with the Holy Spirit, and he is saying the right thing: "Are we on trial for the good deed we did for the sick man?" That is a searching question!

This is the stone which was set at nought of you builders, which is become the head of the corner [Acts 4:11].

Peter goes on to point out two things about the Lord Jesus. The first is that He was crucified and raised from the dead. The other is that Jesus Christ is the stone. Jesus had said, ". . . Upon this rock I will build my church . . ." (Matt. 16:18). What is the rock? The rock is Christ. Now Peter says, "This is the stone." What is the stone? Is it the church, or is it Simon Peter? No, it is the Lord Jesus Christ of Nazareth. He has become the Head of the corner. This has been accomplished by the Resurrection. Notice that the Resurrection is central to the preaching of the Gospel.

> **Neither is there salvation in any other: for there is none other name under heaven given among men, whereby we must be saved [Acts 4:12].**

Go back to the birth of Jesus and the instruction of the angel: ". . . thou shalt call his name JESUS: for he shall save his people from their sins" (Matt. 1:21). He is the Savior. That was His name at the beginning. When you accept the name, you accept all that it implies in the person who is involved. Peter makes it clear, and I want to emphasize that when you come to Him, my friend, you come to Him for salvation. There is no other name under heaven that can save you. The law can't save you. Religion can't save you. A ceremony can't save you. One alone, the name of Jesus, can save you. Jesus is the name of that Person who came down to this earth to save His people from their sins. When any person comes to Him in faith, that person is saved. There is no other place to turn for salvation.

Isn't it interesting that in the long history of this world and all the religions of the world and all the dogmatism that these religions have, not one of them can offer a sure salvation? An uncle of mine was a preacher in a certain church which believes in baptismal regeneration; that is, you must be baptized to be saved. I asked him this question, "Look, if I get baptized as you say, will that guarantee my salvation?" "No," he said, "it couldn't quite do that." My friend, may I say something to you today? There is none other name under heaven whereby you can be saved. If you come to Him, if you trust Christ, then you are saved. That guarantees your salvation.

That was a great message of Simon Peter's, and this is a fine note to conclude that message to the Sanhedrin.

> **Now when they saw the boldness of Peter and John, and perceived that they were unlearned and ignorant men, they marvelled; and they took knowledge of them, that they had been with Jesus [Acts 4:13].**

"Unlearned and ignorant"—that is, these men hadn't been to a theological seminary. But the Sanhedrin noted that they had been with Jesus. How wonderful to have a life that somehow or other calls attention to Jesus!

> **And beholding the man which was healed standing with them, they could say nothing against it.**

> **But when they had commanded them to go aside out of the council, they conferred among themselves [Acts 4:14–15].**

Were they moved by Peter's speech? No, they were not moved at all.

> **Saying, What shall we do to these men? for that indeed a notable miracle hath been done by them is manifest to all them that dwell in Jerusalem; and we cannot deny it [Acts 4:16].**

Not even the Sadducees of that day could deny that a miracle had been performed. It takes a liberal, living in the twentieth century and removed by several thousand miles, to deny miracles. If you had been there then, you would have had difficulty denying the miracle. The liberals of that day had to say, "We cannot deny a miracle has taken place."

People today say that if they could only see a miracle, they would believe. That is not true. This crowd wouldn't believe, and you have the same human nature as these people had. The problem is not a problem of the mind. It is a problem of the will and of the heart. It is the heart that is desperately wicked. Unbelief is not from a lack of facts; it is the condition of the human heart.

Now they are plotting.

> But that it spread no further among the people, let us straitly threaten them, that they speak henceforth to no man in this name.
>
> And they called them, and commanded them not to speak at all or teach in the name of Jesus [Acts 4:17-18].

Peter and John have an answer for them.

> But Peter and John answered and said unto them, Whether it be right in the sight of God to hearken unto you more than unto God, judge ye.
>
> For we cannot but speak the things which we have seen and heard.
>
> So when they had further threatened them, they let them go, finding nothing how they might punish them, because of the people: for all men glorified God for that which was done.
>
> For the man was above forty years old, on whom this miracle of healing was shewed [Acts 4:19-22].

You would think that the men of the Sanhedrin would have been softened by this. They were not. They were hard as nails. Their hearts were hard.

THE POWER OF THE HOLY SPIRIT

> And being let go, they went to their own company, and reported all that the chief priests and elders had said unto them.

> And when they heard that, they lifted up their voice to
> God with one accord, and said, Lord, thou art God,
> which hast made heaven, and earth, and the sea, and
> all that in them is [Acts 4:23–24].

Peter and John have been released and have returned to the church, and they give their report. Here we have recorded a great meeting of the early church. I do not believe the spiritual condition of the church has ever again been on such a high level. We find the key to this in their prayer. It is more than a prayer; it is a song of praise.

"Lord, Thou art God. Lord, You are the Creator." Friend, I am afraid the church is not sure of that today. The Lord is God. Are you sure that the Lord Jesus is God? Are you? That is most important.

The church is not sure today. The church is fumbling; it has lost its power. The church is always talking of methods, always trying this gimmick and that gimmick to attract people. The church in suburbia and the church in downtown are little more than religious clubs. The church is not a powerhouse anymore.

The early church was sure that Jesus is God. They refer to the second psalm:

> Who by the mouth of thy servant David hast said, Why
> did the heathen rage, and the people imagine vain
> things?
>
> The kings of the earth stood up, and the rulers were
> gathered together against the Lord, and against his
> Christ [Acts 4:25–26].

The beginning of the fulfillment of Psalm 2 was when they crucified Jesus Christ. The hatred of Jesus and of God has been snowballing down through the centuries for nineteen hundred years. It is gathering size and momentum. It will finally break into a mighty crescendo upon this earth in the final rebellion of man against God.

> For of a truth against thy holy child Jesus, whom thou
> hast anointed, both Herod, and Pontius Pilate, with the

Gentiles, and the people of Israel, were gathered together,

For to do whatsoever thy hand and thy counsel determined before to be done.

And now, Lord, behold their threatenings: and grant
unto thy servants, that with all boldness they may speak
thy word [Acts 4:27–29].

I am moved by this. This was a great prayer and praise service. They
all were in one accord. Probably they did not all pray at one time, but
they were certainly "amen"-ing the one who led in prayer. Notice that
they did not pray for the persecution to cease. They prayed for the
courage to endure it! They asked for power and for boldness to speak.
That early church was something different, friend, from the church of
our day.

By stretching forth thine hand to heal; and that signs
and wonders may be done by the name of thy holy child
Jesus [Acts 4:30].

Note the power of the early church.

And when they had prayed, the place was shaken where
they were assembled together; and they were all filled
with the Holy Ghost, and they spake the word of God
with boldness [Acts 4:31].

It was the condition of the church which made this possible.

And the multitude of them that believed were of one
heart and of one soul: neither said any of them that
ought of the things which he possessed was his own; but
they had all things common [Acts 4:32].

This did not last very long. Carnality came into the church very soon.

> And with great power gave the apostles witness of the resurrection of the Lord Jesus: and great grace was upon them all [Acts 4:33].

That is the heart of gospel preaching.

> Neither was there any among them that lacked: for as many as were possessors of lands or houses sold them, and brought the prices of the things that were sold,
>
> And laid them down at the apostles' feet: and distribution was made unto every man according as he had need.
>
> And Joses, who by the apostles was surnamed Barnabas, (which is, being interpreted, The son of consolation,) a Levite, and of the country of Cyprus,
>
> Having land, sold it, and brought the money, and laid it at the apostles' feet [Acts 4:34–37].

This kind of living could be carried out for a short while because of the spiritual condition of the church. It is nonsense to say that we should put this into effect today. If we tried it, we would have utter chaos. Why? Because there must first be the same high spiritual level, and we don't have that today. Let us be honest and face up to it. We need to come into a closer relationship to the person of Jesus Christ.

We have been introduced to Barnabas. We will hear more of him later.

CHAPTER 5

THEME: Death of Ananias and Sapphira; second persecution

A s we come to chapter 5, we are continuing to see the effects of the great sermon that Simon Peter gave. Also we are introduced to the first defection in the church, followed by the death of Ananias and Sapphira—who were Christians, but were not living on the high spiritual level of the early church.

At the end of chapter 4 we were introduced to a man by the name of Barnabas. He will be before us again. He was one of the wonderful saints in the early church, a true man of God. He was the first missionary partner of the apostle Paul when they went into the difficult Galatian area, and yet God marvelously blessed their ministry there.

Barnabas had given quite a sum of money to the church. He had made a generous contribution, and everyone was talking about it. I imagine he received a great deal of publicity for his generosity. Remember that in the early church they had all things common. It reveals the fact that they were on a high spiritual level to be able to do this.

Now the first defection comes in. Having all things common could not continue and did not continue simply because of the carnal nature that is in mankind.

DEATH OF ANANIAS AND SAPPHIRA

But a certain man named Ananias, with Sapphira his wife, sold a possession [Acts 5:1].

It is obvious that they were imitating Barnabas. They saw that he got a certain amount of publicity, and they thought it would be nice if they could get that kind of publicity too. They wanted it.

I have found that there are people who will give in order to be noticed. I recall a meeting with businessmen in Pasadena when I was a pastor there. We were planning to start a youth organization, and we were asking these men to give donations for the founding of this movement. It was decided that donations would not be made public.

I was informed that one of these men would contribute very little if he were not given the opportunity to speak out publicly to let everybody know how much he was giving. It is quite interesting that he contributed a small amount. After the meeting he confided in one of the men that he had intended to give about ten times that amount, but he had expected to be able to stand up or at least raise his hand to indicate how much he had given. You see, pride is still in human nature today. That was the condition of Ananias and Sapphira.

> **And kept back part of the price, his wife also being privy to it, and brought a certain part, and laid it at the apostles' feet [Acts 5:2].**

There was nothing wrong with the fact that they kept back part of the money. They had a right to do that. The property had been theirs, and they had the right to do with the money whatever they wished.

Today, we in the church are under grace. We are not constrained to give any certain amount. Someone may say we ought to give a tithe. In the early church they were giving everything they owned. Ananias and Sapphira did not give all but kept back part of it, which they had a right to do. Their problem, their sin, was that they lied about it. They said they were giving all when actually they were keeping part of it for themselves.

I don't like to have people sing the song that talks about putting "my all" on the altar. Unfortunately, that makes liars out of the people who are singing. We need to be very careful about the songs we sing. A vow to the Lord should never be made lightly.

Ananias and Sapphira said they were laying all on the altar, but they were lying about it.

> **But Peter said, Ananias, why hath Satan filled thine heart to lie to the Holy Ghost, and to keep back part of the price of the land? [Acts 5:3].**

The sin of this man and his wife was that they lied about it.

> **Whiles it remained, was it not thine own? and after it
> was sold, was it not in thine own power? why hast thou
> conceived this thing in thine heart? thou hast not lied
> unto men, but unto God [Acts 5:4].**

There are people today who deny that the Holy Spirit is God. You will notice that Simon Peter believed He was God. First he says, "Ananias, why hath Satan filled thine heart to lie to the Holy Ghost?" Then he says, "Thou hast not lied unto men, but unto God." The Holy Spirit is God.

> **And Ananias hearing these words fell down, and gave
> up the ghost: and great fear came on all them that heard
> these things [Acts 5:5].**

There are those today who think that Simon Peter caused the death of this man, Ananias. They even blame him for his death. I want to absolve him of this crime. Simon Peter was probably as much surprised as anyone when Ananias fell down dead. I don't think that he knew at all what was going to happen. Do you know who struck Ananias dead? God did. Do you feel that you want to bring charges against God? Do you want to call the FBI to tell them that God is guilty of murder? May I say to you, if you can give life, you have the right to take it away. This is God's universe. We are God's creatures. We breathe His air. We use bodies that He has given to us. My friend, He can take our bodies any time He wishes to. God is not guilty of a crime. This is *His discipline within the church.* God is the One who is responsible for the death of Ananias and Sapphira.

> **And the young men arose, wound him up, and carried
> him out, and buried him.**

> **And it was about the space of three hours after, when his
> wife, not knowing what was done, came in.**

> And Peter answered unto her, Tell me whether ye sold
> the land for so much? And she said, Yea, for so much.
>
> Then Peter said unto her, How is it that ye have agreed
> together to tempt the Spirit of the Lord? behold, the feet
> of them which have buried thy husband are at the door,
> and shall carry thee out [Acts 5:6-9].

Simon Peter knows what will happen to her. He did not know what was
going to happen to Ananias, but now it is quite obvious what will
happen to this woman.

> Then fell she down straightway at his feet, and yielded
> up the ghost: and the young men came in, and found her
> dead, and, carrying her forth, buried her by her hus-
> band.
>
> And great fear came upon all the church, and upon as
> many as heard these things [Acts 5:10-11].

There are two things that amaze me about this incident. One is the fact
that a lie, such as these two were living, could not exist in the early
church. There was defection in the church, and fear came upon people
who heard of these things. Power would continue in the church, and
multitudes would be saved. Yet the church would never be as pure as
in those first days of existence.

The other amazing thing is the spiritual discernment of Simon
Peter. This also is lacking today.

I was very much amused at a young man who came to me in a Bible
class not long ago. He told me he had the gift of discerning of spirits
and he could tell truth from error. Then he quoted one of the worst
heretics today. I questioned him again about his gifts of discernment of
spirits, of truth and error, and then asked him whether he approved of
the man whom he had just quoted. "Oh yes," he said, "this man
speaks the truth." I told him that I didn't believe he had any special
gift—he just thought he did.

Today the worst kind of hypocrite can get into our Bible churches.

They are not good at coming to Bible studies—I have discovered that, but they can hold offices and even run the church. If those who lied to God in our churches were to drop down dead, we would have a lot of funerals. The undertakers would be doing a land-office business.

> **And by the hands of the apostles were many signs and wonders wrought among the people; (and they were all with one accord in Solomon's porch.**
>
> **And of the rest durst no man join himself to them: but the people magnified them.**
>
> **And believers were the more added to the Lord, multitudes both of men and women.) [Acts 5:12–14].**

Notice that the apostles exercise the apostolic gifts. Gifts of healing and gifts of miracles were sign gifts which were given to the apostles. They did many signs among the people.

The discipline in the church had put a fear on the people and had stopped the revival. Yet there were those who were still being saved. Believers were being added to the Lord. We know that by A.D. 300 there were millions of people in the Roman Empire who had turned to Christ.

> **Insomuch that they brought forth the sick into the streets, and laid them on beds and couches, that at the least the shadow of Peter passing by might overshadow some of them.**
>
> **There came also a multitude out of the cities round about unto Jerusalem, bringing sick folks, and them which were vexed with unclean spirits: and they were healed every one [Acts 5:15–16].**

May I compare this to modern faith healing? Modern faith healers never heal *all* the people who come to them. Have you ever noticed that? The apostles had sign gifts, friend. No one in the church since then has had those gifts. People were healed, every one of them. They emptied the hospitals. This was the power of the early church.

We must remember that at that time there was no written New Testament. The church is built on Jesus Christ—He is the Cornerstone—and the apostles were witnesses to Christ. The sign gifts were given to them to demonstrate the fact that they spoke with God's authority. Today we have a written New Testament as our authority.

THE SECOND PERSECUTION

We have seen that there was discipline within the early church. Now we find that there is persecution from without. When the apostles exercised their gifts, they produced a reaction.

> **Then the high priest rose up, and all they that were with him, (which is the sect of the Sadducees,) and were filled with indignation,**
>
> **And laid their hands on the apostles, and put them in the common prison [Acts 5:17–18].**

Notice that the Sadducees are leading in the persecution. It was the Pharisees who had led in the persecution against Jesus; it is the Sadducees who lead the persecution against the early church. So the apostles are arrested for the second time and are put into prison.

> **But the angel of the Lord by night opened the prison doors, and brought them forth, and said [Acts 5:19].**

This translation should be "*an* angel" and not "*the* angel." In the Old Testament, *the* angel of the Lord was none other than the preincarnate Christ, but now Christ is the Man in glory at God's right hand, and He is the One who is directing the activity of His apostles. Today, unfortunately, much of the time His hands and His feet are paralyzed because the people in the church are not moving for Him in this world. Jesus

Christ wants to move through His church. He wants to move through you and me if we will permit Him. This is not Christ who appeared here; it was an angel.

> **Go, stand and speak in the temple to the people all the words of this life.**
>
> **And when they heard that, they entered into the temple early in the morning, and taught. But the high priest came, and they that were with him, and called the council together, and all the senate of the children of Israel, and sent to the prison to have them brought.**
>
> **But when the officers came, and found them not in the prison, they returned, and told,**
>
> **Saying, The prison truly found we shut with all safety, and the keepers standing without before the doors: but when we had opened, we found no man within [Acts 5:20–23].**

This is the same sort of thing that happened at the resurrection of Christ. The stone wasn't rolled away to let Jesus out; He was out before the stone was rolled away. The stone was moved to let those on the outside come in. The same thing happened here. The doors did not need to be opened to let the apostles get out. They were out long before the doors were unlocked.

> **Now when the high priest and the captain of the temple and the chief priests heard these things, they doubted of them whereunto this would grow.**
>
> **Then came one and told them, saying, Behold, the men whom ye put in prison are standing in the temple, and teaching the people.**
>
> **Then went the captain with the officers, and brought them without violence: for they feared the people, lest they should have been stoned.**

And when they had brought them, they set them before
the council: and the high priest asked them,

Saying, Did not we straitly command you that ye should
not teach in this name? and, behold, ye have filled Jerusalem with your doctrine, and intend to bring this man's
blood upon us [Acts 5:24–28].

People were listening to the apostles. They were good witnesses. They
were real missionaries. Jesus had said that the Gospel was to go out,
first in Jerusalem. We see that this has been done—"Ye have filled Jerusalem with your doctrine."

Then Peter and the other apostles answered and said,
We ought to obey God rather than men [Acts 5:29].

The apostles were obeying what their Lord and Master had told them
to do. Believers are commanded to obey civil authority—except when
it comes in conflict with the commandment of God.

The God of our fathers raised up Jesus, whom ye slew
and hanged on a tree [Acts 5:30].

Jesus Christ was hanged on a tree. It was not a nice, smooth piece of
timber with a crossbar, as we see it pictured today. It was a tree.

Him hath God exalted with his right hand to be a Prince
and a Saviour, for to give repentance to Israel, and for-
giveness of sins.

And we are his witnesses of these things; and so is also
the Holy Ghost, whom God hath given to them that obey
him [Acts 5:31–32].

This is still the message to the nation Israel in Jerusalem today.

When they heard that, they were cut to the heart, and took counsel to slay them.

Then stood there up one in the council, a Pharisee named Gamaliel, a doctor of the law, had in reputation among all the people, and commanded to put the apostles forth a little space [Acts 5:33–34].

Gamaliel wants the apostles excused so that he can talk to the Sanhedrin. This Gamaliel was an outstanding man and greatly respected. (He was the teacher of the apostle Paul, by the way.)

And said unto them, Ye men of Israel, take heed to yourselves what ye intend to do as touching these men.

For before these days rose up Theudas, boasting himself to be somebody; to whom a number of men, about four hundred, joined themselves: who was slain; and all, as many as obeyed him, were scattered, and brought to nought.

After this man rose up Judas of Galilee in the days of the taxing, and drew away much people after him: he also perished; and all, even as many as obeyed him, were dispersed.

And now I say unto you, Refrain from these men, and let them alone: for if this counsel or this work be of men, it will come to nought [Acts 5:35–38].

He is giving sage advice.

But if it be of God, ye cannot overthrow it; lest haply ye be found even to fight against God [Acts 5:39].

Gamaliel gives examples of men who had started uprisings and had a following, but after they were killed, their followers disbanded. Now he advises them that the same thing will happen to Jesus and His followers.

> **And to him they agreed: and when they had called the apostles, and beaten them, they commanded that they should not speak in the name of Jesus, and let them go [Acts 5:40].**

If these men were innocent, they should have let them go. If these men were guilty, they should have held them and punished them. Beating them and then letting them go was a sorry subterfuge. They should have listened to Gamaliel a little more carefully.

Things aren't much different today. There is that gray line between guilty and not guilty. The courts today let people off by giving them some light sentence. My friend, if a person is guilty, he should be punished. If he is not guilty, he should be let go with no sentence.

> **And they departed from the presence of the council, rejoicing that they were counted worthy to suffer shame for his name.**
>
> **And daily in the temple, and in every house, they ceased not to teach and preach Jesus Christ [Acts 5:41–42].**

These apostles were marvelous men. They were rejoicing that they could suffer for the Lord Jesus. They continued to teach and to preach Jesus Christ. What is the Gospel? It is a Person! It is Jesus Christ.

Do you have Him today? You either do or you don't. You either trust Him, or you do not trust Him. Either He is your Savior, or you do not have a Savior. That is the message. The apostles did not cease to teach and to preach Jesus Christ.

CHAPTER 6

THEME: *The appointment of deacons; witness of Stephen, a deacon*

In this chapter we see the further result of the defection that was in the church. We first saw that defection in the case of Ananias and Sapphira. They were believers who were saved, but they could not remain in the early church with that lie in their lives.

Now the defection we see in this chapter led to the selection of deacons. The chapter continues with the account of one of those deacons, Stephen. He was framed, arrested, and tried.

THE APPOINTMENT OF DEACONS

And in those days, when the number of the disciples was multiplied, there arose a murmuring of the Grecians against the Hebrews, because their widows were neglected in the daily ministration [Acts 6:1].

We need to recognize that this took place early in the history of the church. They had attempted a form of communal living and, actually, it succeeded for a short while. Then carnality entered the church. We saw how Ananias and Sapphira misrepresented their situation. Now we find that there is a murmuring of the Grecians against the Hebrews. This is not a clash between two races. This is not a demonstration of anti-Semitism. The word *Grecians* here means "Hellenists," Greek-speaking Jews. They had a background of Greek culture while the Hebrews in Jerusalem closely followed the Mosaic Law. Naturally, a misunderstanding developed.

It has been estimated that the number in the church at this time may have been around twenty-five thousand. And we see that this early church was not perfect. We hear people say, "We need to get back to the early church. The early church was power-conscious, and we

today are problem-conscious." That is only a half-truth. The early
church did have power, but the early church had problems also.

The high plane to which the Spirit had brought the church was
interrupted by the intrusion of satanic division and confusion. The
sharing of material substance, which first characterized the church,
gave way to the selfishness of the old nature. Carnality had come in.
The Grecians, who evidently were a minority group, felt neglected and
demanded that their widows be given equal consideration with the
Hebrews. This communal form of living wasn't working as well as
they would have liked. This was brought to the attention of the apostles.

> **Then the twelve called the multitude of the disciples
> unto them, and said, It is not reason that we should
> leave the word of God, and serve tables [Acts 6:2].**

The apostles felt that they should not give up the study of the Word of
God. They felt it was important for them to continue with that. If they
gave up the study of the Word of God and served tables, that would be
the undoing of them. They *should* spend their time in prayer and in
the study of the Word of God.

It is important for every church to recognize that the minister
should have time to study the Word of God and should have time for
prayer. Unfortunately, the average church today is looking for a pastor
who is an organizer and a promoter, a sort of vice-president to run the
church, a manager of some sort. That is unfortunate. As a result the
church is suffering today. When I was a pastor in downtown Los
Angeles, I had to move my study to my home. I built a special room
over the garage for my study. I found out that all I had in the church
was an office, not a study. They didn't intend for me to study there.

> **Wherefore, brethren, look ye out among you seven men
> of honest report, full of the Holy Ghost and wisdom,
> whom we may appoint over this business.**
>
> **But we will give ourselves continually to prayer, and to
> the ministry of the word [Acts 6:3-4].**

The seven men were to be appointed because a crisis had arisen. The apostles felt it was important that they should not have the burden of this detail so that they could give themselves to prayer and the ministry of the Word.

Now I want you to notice the qualifications of these seven men who are to assume the burden of handling the material substance of the church. I'm afraid this is something which is neglected in the average church today when the deacons are chosen. In fact, I've heard men say they didn't want to be appointed to the spiritual office of an elder but would like to be a deacon to handle the material things.

May I say to you, the office of deacon requires more spirituality and wisdom and prayer than any other office. Now notice the qualifications: These men had to be men of honest report. Their honesty was to be unquestionable. It is really a tragic thing for a church to have a deacon whose honesty is in question so that others—including the pastor—cannot trust him. Such a man should not be in the office of deacon. The second qualification was "full of the Holy Ghost." They were not to be filled with wine but were to be "filled with the [Holy] Spirit" (Eph. 5:18). Thirdly, they were to be men of wisdom. They were to be spiritual men who would be able to make an application of spiritual truth. That was very important. You see, the fact that they were handling material matters was apt to give them a lopsided view of things. So it is most important that deacons should be men who look at things from the spiritual point of view.

We shall see that Stephen was a man who met these qualifications. He had wisdom—"they were not able to resist the wisdom and the spirit by which he spake" (v. 10). He had real conviction. Also he was "full of faith." Not only did he have saving faith but also serving faith—witnessing faith. It wasn't the amount of his faith but the object of his faith that was important. We learn from this same verse that he was full of power. Such were the kind of men chosen as deacons.

But we will give ourselves continually to prayer, and to the ministry of the word [Acts 6:4].

That was the duty of the apostles.

> And the saying pleased the whole multitude: and they
> chose Stephen, a man full of faith and of the Holy Ghost,
> and Philip, and Prochorus, and Nicanor, and Timon,
> and Parmenas, and Nicolas a proselyte of Antioch [Acts
> 6:5].

I can't tell you anything more about the last five men. The first two,
Stephen and Philip, will be mentioned again as we go along in the
Book of Acts. They were outstanding men in the early church. Although they were to "serve tables," the record of them is that they were
spiritual men.

> Whom they set before the apostles: and when they had
> prayed, they laid their hands on them [Acts 6:6].

Now, friends, there is a great deal of hocus-pocus and abracadabra connected with this matter of laying on of hands. A great many people
think that some spiritual power is connected to it. They think that putting on the hands communicates something to a person. Frankly, the
only thing you can communicate to someone else by the laying on of
hands is disease germs. You can pass them on, but you cannot pass on
any kind of power.

What is the meaning of the laying on of hands? As we saw in Leviticus, when we were studying the Old Testament sacrifices, the sinner
would put his hand on the head of the animal to be sacrificed, which
signified that the animal to be offered was taking his place. The offering was identified with the sinner.

When the apostles put their hands on the heads of the deacons, it
meant that now the deacons would be partners with them. They were
together in this service. It designated that these men were set aside for
this office, denoting their fellowship in the things of Christ and their
position as representatives for the corporate body of believers.

Notice that this was a social service in which these men were engaged. The early church took care of its own. I think that should still
be true today. The early church had a poverty program, and it included

only the members of the church. The church today should also take care of its own.

> **And the word of God increased; and the number of the disciples multiplied in Jerusalem greatly; and a great company of the priests were obedient to the faith [Acts 6:7].**

It is still important in our day for the Word of God to be increasing. Certainly this is the purpose of my radio program. It is my sincere desire that the Word of God may be increased.

Don't miss the fact that many of the priests turned to the Lord. Some of them must have been serving in the temple when the veil was rent in two at the death of Christ. Many of them must have turned to Christ after that experience.

WITNESS OF STEPHEN, A DEACON

Our attention is now drawn to Stephen. He is one of the great men in the early church.

> **And Stephen, full of faith and power, did great wonders and miracles among the people [Acts 6:8].**

Apparently these deacons are one with the apostles in having the sign gifts. They have been brought into a unique position. Because Stephen is a strong witness to the Gospel, he incurs the hatred of the Sadducees. False witnesses are brought before the council to accuse Stephen.

> **Then there arose certain of the synagogue, which is called the synagogue of the Libertines, and Cyrenians, and Alexandrians, and of them of Cilicia and of Asia, disputing with Stephen.**
>
> **And they were not able to resist the wisdom and the spirit by which he spake.**

Then they suborned men, which said, We have heard him speak blasphemous words against Moses, and against God.

And they stirred up the people, and the elders, and the scribes, and came upon him, and caught him, and brought him to the council,

And set up false witnesses, which said, This man ceaseth not to speak blasphemous words against this holy place, and the law:

For we have heard him say, that this Jesus of Nazareth shall destroy this place, and shall change the customs which Moses delivered us.

And all that sat in the council, looking stedfastly on him, saw his face as it had been the face of an angel [Acts 6:9–15].

Stephen is brought before the Sanhedrin, and false witnesses are brought in. The false witnesses tell a half-truth, of course. The Lord Jesus did say that they would destroy this temple and He would raise it up again, but He was speaking of the temple of His body. At His trial, the false witnesses misunderstood that and misrepresented it. So here, they misunderstand Stephen when he says that the temple in Jerusalem will be left desolate. Actually, it was desolate without Christ anyway. And they twist what he is saying about the customs of Moses. Of course men are not saved by the Law but by grace. But salvation in Moses' day was by grace even as it is today. Their accusation is based on only a partial truth.

They see something marvelous in the face of Stephen. This man came closer to being an angel than any man who has ever lived.

CHAPTER 7

THEME: Stephen's address and martyrdom

In this chapter we find Stephen's defense before the council—which is really not a defense. Rather it is a rehearsal of the history of the nation Israel and of their resistance and rebellion against God. He charges the council of being betrayers and murderers of Jesus. That, of course, engenders their bitterest hatred and leads to the stoning of Stephen.

In his inspired survey of the history of the nation, Stephen makes it very clear that there never was a time when the entire nation worshipped God. Yet there was always the believing remnant, a small remnant of true believers—even as there is in our day.

STEPHEN'S ADDRESS

Then said the high priest, Are these things so?

And he said, Men, brethren, and fathers, hearken; The God of glory appeared unto our father Abraham, when he was in Mesopotamia, because he dwelt in Charran [Acts 7:1–2].

They have made an accusation against him. He is questioned as to the truth of the charges. In his response he makes no attempt to clear himself. In fact, he doesn't even mention the charges they have made against him.

What a marvelous beginning. He calls them *brethren*. They are his brethren in the flesh. He calls the older men *fathers*. He is a younger man and shows them this respect. This young man is to become the first martyr in the church.

We sometimes hear it said that at the beginning Christianity was actually a youth movement. It is not altogether inaccurate to state that it was a youth movement. Two men who held as prominent a place as any were Stephen and Saul of Tarsus, whom we will meet soon. These two men had a great deal to do with the shaping of the course of the early church. Both of them were remarkable young men. Both of them were gifted and used by the Holy Spirit. Yet the only time these two young men ever met, they were enemies. The cross divided Stephen and Saul of Tarsus just as truly as it divided the two thieves who were crucified with Jesus. Paul knew what he was saying in 1 Corinthians 1:18: "For the preaching of the cross is to them that perish foolishness; but unto us which are saved it is the power of God." When Saul saw Stephen, he thought Stephen was very foolish.

This address of Stephen is a master stroke. He reviews the history of the nation beginning with Abraham. That is where the history of the nation Israel began. They did not go back any farther. You will find the same thing in the Gospel of Matthew. This book, written to the nation Israel, traces the genealogy of Jesus Christ back to Abraham. If you want to trace it all the way back to Adam, you must turn to the Gospel of Luke. Stephen starts with Abraham, a man of faith.

Even though he traces the resistance and rebellion against God by the nation, still there was always a believing remnant.

This is true today, too. In the organized church, in the visible church which you and I can see, there is a remnant of believers. Not every one in the visible church is a true believer. People may ask, "Do you think So-and-So is a Christian?" The answer is that even though he goes to church and is a church officer, he may not be a Christian. Just as in the nation Israel there was the believing remnant, so in the visible church there is the little remnant of true believers.

Abraham was a man of faith. He believed God, and he obeyed God. Faith always leads to obedience. Stephen starts his narrative with Abraham in Mesopotamia, down in the Tigris-Euphrates valley. That was the place of Abraham's hometown. It was there that God called him.

And said unto him, Get thee out of thy country, and from thy kindred, and come into the land which I shall shew thee [Acts 7:3].

God called Abraham away from his home because it was a home of idolatry.

> Then came he out of the land of Chaldaeans, and dwelt in Charran: and from thence, when his father was dead, he removed him into this land, wherein ye now dwell.
>
> And he gave him none inheritance in it, no, not so much as to set his foot on: yet he promised that he would give it to him for a possession, and to his seed after him, when as yet he had no child [Acts 7:4–5].

He is relating the story of Abraham. This shows the faith of Abraham. God had promised him a child, and God had promised him the land. Although Abraham had neither one, he believed God.

> And God spake on this wise, That his seed should sojourn in a strange land; and that they should bring them into bondage, and entreat them evil four hundred years.
>
> And the nation to whom they shall be in bondage will I judge, said God: and after that shall they come forth, and serve me in this place.
>
> And he gave him the covenant of circumcision: and so Abraham begat Isaac, and circumcised him the eighth day; and Isaac begat Jacob; and Jacob begat the twelve patriarchs [Acts 7:6–8].

Stephen goes from Abraham to the patriarchal period. He speaks of the brethren of Joseph, motivated by envy and hatred who sold Joseph into Egypt. But God overruled and used Joseph to save them. What we have here is really the Spirit's interpretation of the Old Testament. That makes this a remarkable section.

> And the patriarchs, moved with envy, sold Joseph into Egypt: but God was with him,

And delivered him out of all his afflictions, and gave him favour and wisdom in the sight of Pharaoh king of Egypt; and he made him governor over Egypt and all his house.

Now there came a dearth over all the land of Egypt and Chanaan, and great affliction: and our fathers found no sustenance.

But when Jacob heard that there was corn in Egypt, he sent out our fathers first.

And at the second time Joseph was made known to his brethren; and Joseph's kindred was made known unto Pharaoh.

Then sent Joseph, and called his father Jacob to him, and all his kindred, threescore and fifteen souls.

So Jacob went down into Egypt, and died, he, and our fathers,

And were carried over into Sychem, and laid in the sepulchre that Abraham bought for a sum of money of the sons of Emmor the father of Sychem [Acts 7:9–16].

Now Stephen comes to another period in the history of these people. He is going to remind them of the deliverance out of Egypt. God made Moses the deliverer. And he shows that at first the children of Israel refused to follow Moses and that Moses had trouble with them all the way.

But when the time of the promise drew nigh, which God had sworn to Abraham, the people grew and multiplied in Egypt,

Till another king arose, which knew not Joseph.

The same dealt subtilly with our kindred, and evil entreated our fathers, so that they cast out their young children, to the end they might not live.

> In which time Moses was born, and was exceeding fair,
> and nourished up in his father's house three months:
>
> And when he was cast out, Pharaoh's daughter took him
> up, and nourished him for her own son [Acts 7:17-21].

The comment which Stephen adds confirms some of the things that we said when we were studying about Moses. If Rameses II was the pharaoh of the oppression, Moses could have been the next pharaoh. Pharaoh's daughter brought him up as her own son. This pharaoh had no sons, so Moses would have been the next in line.

> And Moses was learned in all the wisdom of the Egyptians, and was mighty in words and in deeds [Acts 7:22].

Moses was brought up in the wisdom of the Egyptians. The wisdom of the Egyptians is not despised even in our advanced day when we feel that we know about everything. Too often we do not give the Egyptians full credit for what they did know. They had developed mathematics, chemistry, engineering, architecture, and astronomy to a very fine point. They had developed these fields of study in a way that was really remarkable. Look at the pyramids. Look at the colors we find in the tombs, colors which have stood the test of the centuries. They understood about embalming. They had calculated the distance to the sun. My friend, they had a highly developed culture and were not an ignorant people.

Moses had all the advantage of that day, being raised as the son of Pharaoh's daughter. He was learned in all the wisdom of the Egyptians. He was outstanding. Yet he was not prepared to lead God's people. All the learning of the world of that day did not equip him to lead God's people. All the wisdom that men have today is not enough for them to understand the Word of God. It is too difficult. Why? Because the natural man cannot receive the things of the Spirit of God. These things are foolishness to him and he cannot know them because they are spiritually discerned (see 1 Cor. 2:14). Although Moses was learned in the wisdom of his day, he was not ready to deliver God's people. So, after forty years of learning in Egypt, God put him out into the desert. There God gave him his B.D. degree, his Backside of the Desert degree, and prepared him to become the deliverer.

> **And when he was full forty years old, it came into his heart to visit his brethren the children of Israel.**

> **And seeing one of them suffer wrong, he defended him, and avenged him that was oppressed, and smote the Egyptian:**

> **For he supposed his brethren would have understood how that God by his hand would deliver them: but they understood not [Acts 7:23–25].**

Notice that Moses did what he considered to be a very fine thing to do. He intended to deliver his brethren. But they didn't understand. Actually, neither did Moses understand. He still was not really ready, and God had to take him out to the desert to train him.

> **And the next day he shewed himself unto them as they strove, and would have set them at one again, saying, Sirs, ye are brethren; why do ye wrong one to another?**

> **But he that did his neighbour wrong thrust him away, saying, Who made thee a ruler and a judge over us?**

> **Wilt thou kill me, as thou didest the Egyptian yesterday? [Acts 7:26–28].**

Now Moses was frightened.

> **Then fled Moses at this saying, and was a stranger in the land of Madian, where he begat two sons.**

> **And when forty years were expired, there appeared to him in the wilderness of mount Sina an angel of the Lord in a flame of fire in a bush.**

> When Moses saw it, he wondered at the sight: and as he
> drew near to behold it, the voice of the Lord came unto
> him [Acts 7:29-31].

Moses had wanted to deliver the children of Israel, but he wasn't prepared for it, and the people weren't prepared for him either. They
wouldn't accept his leadership. They resisted him. Then God called
him to be the deliverer.

> Saying, I am the God of thy fathers, the God of Abra-
> ham, and the God of Isaac, and the God of Jacob. Then
> Moses trembled, and durst not behold.

> Then said the Lord to him, Put off thy shoes from they
> feet: for the place where thou standest is holy ground.

> I have seen, I have seen the affliction of my people
> which is in Egypt, and I have heard their groaning, and
> am come down to deliver them. And now come, I will
> send thee into Egypt [Acts 7:32-34].

God told Moses, "I have heard their groaning." He saw their need.
That was the reason He delivered them. It was for the same reason that
He provided a Savior for you and me. It wasn't because we are such
wonderful people. He didn't look down and say, "My, they are so
lovely down there. I must go down and save them. They are so sweet,
and so kind, and so loving to Me, and so faithful to Me." No! God
looked down and saw nothing but corrupt, rotten sinners. We were all
lost in iniquity. He loved us in spite of our unloveliness. That is the
explanation.

> This Moses whom they refused, saying, Who made thee
> a ruler and a judge? the same did God send to be a ruler
> and a deliverer by the hand of the angel which appeared
> to him in the bush [Acts 7:35].

Notice the emphasis that has been placed upon the ministry of the
angels in the life of the nation Israel. You will find the ministry of

angels prominent throughout Israel's history. God gave the Law to Moses through the ministry of angels.

We hear a lot about the angels at Christmas. Whom were the angels addressing? And for what purpose? They had messages for the people of Israel—for Mary, for Joseph, for Zacharias, and for the shepherds.

God is not sending messages through angels during this period of the church. No angels have appeared around my place. And there have been none appearing to you. If you are seeing angels, you had better make an appointment with a psychiatrist. By contrast, angels did appear and bring messages from God to members of the nation Israel.

Now Stephen goes on to describe the wilderness experience.

> He brought them out, after that he had shewed wonders and signs in the land of Egypt, and in the Red sea, and in the wilderness forty years.

> This is that Moses, which said unto the children of Israel, A prophet shall the Lord your God raise up unto you of your brethren, like unto me; him shall ye hear.

> This is he, that was in the church in the wilderness with the angel which spake to him in the mount Sina, and with our fathers: who received the lively oracles to give unto us [Acts 7:36–38].

The word church here does not mean that there was a church in the Old Testament in the same sense that there is a church in the New Testament. The word for church is ekklésia, which means "called-out." Even a group called out to mob somebody would be an ekklésia, a called-out group. So, Israel in the wilderness was a called-out group. They were called out of Egypt, by God, for a particular purpose.

> To whom our fathers would not obey, but thrust him from them, and in their hearts turned back again into Egypt [Acts 7:39].

Israel did not go back to Egypt in a physical, material sense. But in their hearts they went back to Egypt many, many times. In the same way there are many people today who say they deplore certain sins of the world and sins of the flesh. It is always so easy to point the finger at someone else and condemn him for his sin. A question we need to ask ourselves is: Would I *like* to do the same thing? Where is our heart? Israel went back to Egypt in their heart.

> **Saying unto Aaron, Make us gods to go before us: for as for this Moses, which brought us out of the land of Egypt, we wot not what is become of him [Acts 7:40].**

They didn't know what had happened to him, and they didn't care. They had rejected Moses.

> **And they made a calf in those days, and offered sacrifice unto the idols, and rejoiced in the works of their own hands [Acts 7:41].**

Stephen is showing them that Israel has always been rebellious.

> **Then God turned, and gave them up to worship the host of heaven; as it is written in the book of the prophets, O ye house of Israel, have ye offered to me slain beasts and sacrifices by the space of forty years in the wilderness? [Acts 7:42].**

They went into idolatry. That is why Moses (and later Joshua) pleaded with the people to choose God and turn from their idols.

> **Yea, ye took up the tabernacle of Moloch, and the star of your god Remphan, figures which ye made to worship them: and I will carry you away beyond Babylon.**

> **Our fathers had the tabernacle of witness in the wilderness, as he had appointed, speaking unto Moses, that he should make it according to the fashion that he had seen.**

> Which also our fathers that came after brought in with
> Jesus into the possession of the Gentiles, whom God
> drave out before the face of our fathers, unto the days of
> David [Acts 7:43–45].

Jesus is the Greek translation of the Hebrew name *Joshua*.

> Who found favour before God, and desired to find a tab-
> ernacle for the God of Jacob [Acts 7:46].

You see that the temple was David's idea. I have always thought it
should be called David's temple even though Solomon built it.

> But Solomon built him an house.
>
> Howbeit the most High dwelleth not in temples made
> with hands; as saith the prophet,
>
> Heaven is my throne, and earth is my footstool: what
> house will ye build me? saith the Lord: or what is the
> place of my rest?
>
> Hath not my hand made all these things? [Acts
> 7:47–50].

Now he comes to his condemnation of the religious rulers of that day.

> Ye stiffnecked and uncircumcised in heart and ears, ye
> do always resist the Holy Ghost: as your fathers did, so
> do ye.
>
> Which of the prophets have not your fathers persecuted?
> and they have slain them which shewed before of the
> coming of the Just One; of whom ye have been now the
> betrayers and murderers:

Who have received the law by the disposition of angels, and have not kept it [Acts 7:51–53].

Physically, these men were circumcised, but in their hearts and in their ears, they were uncircumcised. That is, they would not hear God any more than their ancestors down through the years had heard Him.

This is a masterful speech. Stephen reminds them of the deliverance out of Egypt. God made Moses the deliverer, but the children of Israel refused to obey him. The wilderness experience was a series of rebellions against God, brought to a climax in the making of a golden calf. A plague of idolatry broke out again in the land and resulted in the Babylonian captivity. Stephen concludes with Joshua, who led them into the land, and Jesus, who made the way to heaven. He charges that the Law was given to them supernaturally by the ministry of angels, and they did not keep it. Perhaps they knew that the birth of Jesus was announced by angels. Obviously, they have been the betrayers and murderers of Him.

MARTYRDOM OF STEPHEN

Stephen became the first martyr. Also, in this portion of the chapter, we are first introduced to Saul of Tarsus.

When they heard these things, they were cut to the heart, and they gnashed on him with their teeth [Acts 7:54].

How they hated Stephen for saying what he did!

But he, being full of the Holy Ghost, looked up stedfastly into heaven, and saw the glory of God, and Jesus standing on the right hand of God [Acts 7:55].

Since God is a spirit, how can there be a right hand of God? Because at "the right hand of God" indicates the place of prominence, the place of honor. God had promised Jesus Christ that He would glorify Him and give Him a name that is above every name. Jesus Christ is exalted. He is at the right hand of God. In Hebrews 1:3 we are told, ". . . when he had by himself purged our sins, sat down on the right hand of the Majesty on high." The fact that He was *seated* at the right hand of God indicates that His work was completed—our redemption is finished. But that doesn't mean He isn't still working in our behalf. Here He is standing, ready to receive His first martyr.

> **And said, Behold, I see the heavens opened, and the Son of man standing on the right hand of God.**

> **Then they cried out with a loud voice, and stopped their ears, and ran upon him with one accord,**

> **And cast him out of the city, and stoned him: and the witnesses laid down their clothes at a young man's feet, whose name was Saul [Acts 7:56–58].**

These two young men—Stephen and Saul of Tarsus—are together here for the first time, the only time, the last time. They are enemies. They stand on the opposite sides of the cross.

> **And they stoned Stephen, calling upon God, and saying, Lord Jesus, receive my spirit.**

> **And he kneeled down, and cried with a loud voice, Lord, lay not this sin to their charge. And when he had said this, he fell asleep [Acts 7:59–60].**

Stephen falls asleep. Jesus puts his body to sleep to await the Rapture. Stephen goes into the presence of Christ who is standing to meet him. Stephen is the first martyr of the church to go to be with his Lord.
The other young man there that day was a Pharisee, and he thought

he had everything. He looked up into heaven when Stephen said that he saw the heavens open. I am sure that Saul looked up longingly and admitted to himself, *I don't see anything, but I'd like to see what he sees. I have an empty heart.* Stephen was a tremendous witness to Saul. Stephen was the one, I believe, who prepared Saul for the appearance of the Lord Jesus on the Damascus road, as we shall see.

CHAPTER 8

THEME: Conversion of Ethiopian eunuch (son of Ham)

We have now arrived at the second major division of the Book of Acts. You remember that we divided the book according to the Lord's commission in Acts 1:8. First they were to witness in Jerusalem. Now we come to the Lord Jesus Christ's work by the Holy Spirit through the apostles in Judea and Samaria. This section of the book includes chapters 8—12.

Chapter 7 concluded with a most unusual scene. It included the two young men who had the greatest influence upon the early church. The one was Stephen, the deacon, the young man who gave up his life, the first martyr in the church. That other was a young Pharisee who had charge of the stoning of Stephen. His name was Saul.

SAUL BECOMES THE CHIEF PERSECUTOR OF THE CHURCH, AND THE CHURCH IS SCATTERED

And Saul was consenting unto his death. And at that time there was a great persecution against the church which was at Jerusalem; and they were all scattered abroad throughout the regions of Judaea and Samaria, except the apostles [Acts 8:1].

Saul was taking the lead in the persecution of Stephen, and he was in the cheering section. Now this young man, Saul of Tarsus, was amazed when he saw the face of Stephen. Stephen was looking into the heavens, and there he saw the Son of Man standing at the right hand of God. Young Saul looked up—he didn't see anything. But, friend, he wished he could. He will see a little later. I believe that Stephen is the one who prepared Saul for the appearance of the Lord Jesus on the Damascus road.

Saul becomes the chief persecutor of the church. This causes the church to scatter. Actually, he does the church a favor. They were all settled down in Jerusalem, and I don't think they would have moved out had it not been for the persecution which Saul of Tarsus instigated.

Judea and Samaria are the next territories which the Lord had told them to enter. Judea surrounds Jerusalem, and Samaria lies to the north of Jerusalem.

And devout men carried Stephen to his burial, and made great lamentation over him [Acts 8:2].

I would like to make a few remarks here about Christian burial. There is a question that comes to us today: Is it right or wrong for Christians to be cremated? There is nothing in the Bible against it. No one will lose salvation by being cremated. However, the burial of a Christian is like sowing weeds. It is like putting the body into a motel so it can sleep until the resurrection.

This is the way Paul speaks of it in 1 Thessalonians 4. He speaks of the body as seed in 1 Corinthians 15. You don't burn the seed before you plant it. Neither do you burn a person before you put him into a motel or hotel to go to sleep. Planting the body in the earth like a seed is a testimony—an evidence of your faith in a future resurrection. Undoubtedly the body of Stephen was terribly mutilated. They took him up tenderly and put him in the ground as you would plant a seed. Stephen had gone into the presence of Christ, who was waiting in heaven for him. His body went into the ground to await the resurrection. "So also is the resurrection of the dead. It is sown in corruption; it is raised in incorruption: It is sown in dishonour; it is raised in glory: it is sown in weakness; it is raised in power: it is sown a natural body; it is raised a spiritual body. There is a natural body, and there is a spiritual body" (1 Cor. 15:42–44). I cannot see that cremation sets forth this idea. Rather, this is the picture of real Christian burial.

Some people protest that we are running out of space for graves. My friend, this old earth has taken in bodies for thousands of years now, and there is still room.

As for Saul, he made havoc of the church, entering into
every house, and haling men and women committed
them to prison [Acts 8:3].

This was a young man full of zeal. Remember that he later wrote about
himself—"Concerning zeal, persecuting the church . . ." in Philippians 3:6.

Therefore they that were scattered abroad went every
where preaching the word [Acts 8:4].

Here we see the effect of the persecution. Actually, it did not hinder the
church but furthered the work of the church. Later on, Paul would give
this same kind of testimony after he had been put into prison in Rome,
"But I would ye should understand, brethren, that the things which
happened unto me have fallen out rather unto the furtherance of the
gospel" (Phil. 1:12). I do not believe that the church can ever be hurt
from the outside. It can be hurt from the inside, as we shall see later in
this chapter.

PHILIP BECOMES THE CHIEF WITNESS AFTER
THE DEATH OF STEPHEN

We are introduced to the second deacon whom God used in a marvelous way.

Then Philip went down to the city of Samaria, and
preached Christ unto them [Acts 8:5].

The Lord Jesus had said they should be witnesses unto Him in Jerusalem and Judea and Samaria. Now the Word is going to Samaria.

And the people with one accord gave heed unto those
things which Philip spake, hearing and seeing the miracles which he did [Acts 8:6].

Stephen had had the sign gifts of the early church, and now we see that
Philip had those same gifts. Not everyone had them—only those who
were in the places of leadership, those who were taking the Word of
God out to the world. There came the day when the sign gifts disappeared. They disappeared after the time of the apostles. By the time
the canon of Scripture was complete and established, the credentials of
a true man of God was correct doctrine rather than sign gifts.

> **For unclean spirits, crying with loud voice, came out of
> many that were possessed with them: and many taken
> with palsies, and that were lame, were healed.**
>
> **And there was great joy in that city [Acts 8:7–8].**

The Gospel has now come to Samaria. Philip is well received in Samaria, and there, of all places, the Gospel brings great joy.

Now because the church is growing very fast, there are people actually joining the church who are not believers. Although they are
really unbelievers, they make a profession of faith. We will now meet
one like that.

SIMON THE SORCERER

> **But there was a certain man, called Simon, which be-
> foretime in the same city used sorcery, and bewitched
> the people of Samaria, giving out that himself was some
> great one [Acts 8:9].**

He sets himself up as some great one. We find the same sort of thing
today. If someone claims to be a faith healer, that sets him apart, believe me. People may declare that the faith healers are humble. Humility is not manifest in services where a person is supposedly healing
people and implying that he is the only person there who has that gift.
That is "giving out that himself was some great one," as Simon the
sorcerer was doing.

To whom they all gave heed, from the least to the greatest, saying, This man is the great power of God.

And to him they had regard, because that of long time
he had bewitched them with sorceries [Acts 8:10–11].

These people felt that Simon the sorcerer was like a god. Just as with
these people, there are a great many people who are bewitched today.
My friend, do not be bewitched by any man or his power. Even if a man
is giving out the Word of God, do not look to the man. Look to the Word
of God and check to see if he is presenting it accurately. Look to God.
Turn to Him. When we get our eyes on man, we take our eyes off the
Lord Jesus Christ. That is what had happened in Samaria.

But when they believed Philip preaching the things concerning the kingdom of God, and the name of Jesus
Christ, they were baptized, both men and women [Acts
8:12].

Philip preached the Gospel in Samaria, and many men and women
believed. Simon came in contact with Philip, and apparently he made
a profession of faith under the ministry of Philip. I believe that Simon
is the first religious racketeer in the church—but, unfortunately, not
the last. He professes to be a believer during the sweeping revival in
Samaria under the ministry of Philip.

Then Simon himself believed also: and when he was
baptized, he continued with Philip, and wondered, beholding the miracles and signs which were done [Acts
8:13].

Simon believes, he is baptized, and he becomes a friend of Philip. You
would certainly think he was a real child of God. However, he is not
converted. We will see that there are also others who are professing
believers, but they are not born again. They have the head knowledge,
they go along with the crowd, but they are not saved. Although they
have been baptized with water, they have not been baptized into the
church of Jesus Christ by the Holy Spirit.

There are a great many people like that today. I receive many letters from people who have told me that since they have been studying the Bible along with our program, they have begun to examine their faith. Many have come to realize that they have just been following along with someone else and that they have not been genuinely, personally converted. Paul says, "Examine yourselves, whether ye be in the faith; prove your own selves . . ." (2 Cor. 13:5). It is a very good thing to check yourself. See whether you are in the faith or not.

This man Simon had all the outward trappings. He answered that he did believe in Jesus, and so he was baptized. But it was not a genuine faith.

> **Now when the apostles which were at Jerusalem heard that Samaria had the word of God, they sent unto them Peter and John:**
>
> **Who, when they were come down, prayed for them, that they might receive the Holy Ghost:**
>
> **(For as yet he was fallen upon none of them: only they were baptized in the name of Lord Jesus.) [Acts 8:14–16].**

When the apostles heard that there was a great moving of the Spirit down in Samaria, they sent Peter and John to check on it. They found a great company of professing believers who had not been born again. They had not been baptized into the church by the Holy Spirit. They were not saved. They had gone through an outward ceremony.

My friend, being baptized with water or going through some other ceremony will not make you a Christian. This gives the background to explain why Simon was able to put over his racket on the others. He liked this idea of performing miracles.

> **Then laid they their hands on them, and they received the Holy Ghost [Acts 8:17].**

It may be that Philip had not told all the facts and conditions of the Gospel. It may be that they had not accepted them. At any rate, now they are brought into partnership with the apostles. Now they believe the Gospel, and they believe in the Lord Jesus Christ. Now the Spirit of God has entered into them. I think this needs to be considered in its historical setting. It was the commission given to the apostles to open up each new area to the Gospel. On the Day of Pentecost the Gospel was given in Jerusalem. Peter and John are to bring it into Samaria and Judea. Paul is to be the apostle to the Gentiles. Jesus had given this commission. We are now seeing it fulfilled here in Samaria.

> **And when Simon saw that through laying on of the apostles' hands the Holy Ghost was given, he offered them money.**
>
> **Saying, Give me also this power, that on whomsoever I lay hands, he may receive the Holy Ghost [Acts 8:18–19].**

Simon wanted to pay for the gift. Why? Well, because this man is a religious racketeer. He wants to see it for profit.

How many such claims are made by individuals today! They claim that great miracles take place in their meetings and humbly say they have nothing to do with them. If that is so, why do they permit this type of deception to go on? *Bewitch* is the word used here. There have been religious racketeers around bewitching the multitudes from that day to this.

Persecution from the outside didn't hurt the church. It scattered the believers and actually worked for the furtherance of the Gospel. What hurt the church was that people got on the inside, professing to be believers when they were not believers. Always the church is hurt from the inside.

It was the same with the Lord Jesus. He was betrayed from the inside. He was betrayed to His nation by one of His own disciples. His own nation betrayed Him to the Roman Empire, and the Roman Empire crucified Him. Also today He is betrayed within the church.

It is like the wooden horse brought into the city of Troy. The city was impenetrable, it was invulnerable, until that wooden horse got on the inside. The Devil started out by persecuting the church, fighting it from the outside. He found that didn't work. It just spread the Gospel. Then he decided to start his work from the inside. That is where he can get in and do damage. How many pastors could testify to that today!

> **But Peter said unto him, Thy money perish with thee, because thou hast thought that the gift of God may be purchased with money.**

> **Thou hast neither part nor lot in this matter: for thy heart is not right in the sight of God [Acts 8:20–21].**

This is the reason we know this man is not converted. Simon Peter declares that his heart is not right with God. He is not converted. His big interest is in the money. That was the important thing to this man.

> **Repent therefore of this thy wickedness, and pray God, if perhaps the thought of thine heart may be forgiven thee.**

> **For I perceive that thou art in the gall of bitterness, and in the bond of iniquity [Acts 8:22–23].**

You can't make it any stronger than the way Simon Peter says it.

> **Then answered Simon, and said, Pray ye to the Lord for me, that none of these things which ye have spoken come upon me [Acts 8:24].**

Simon doesn't ask to be saved. He doesn't ask for prayer for his salvation. He just asks that none of those terrible things happen to him. We do not know if this man ever came to Christ.

> **And they, when they had testified and preached the word of the Lord, returned to Jerusalem, and preached the Gospel in many villages of the Samaritans [Acts 8:25].**

The Gospel is starting its journey to the ends of the earth. It started in Jerusalem. The apostles were there and a church was established. Soon the center will move to Antioch. Then it will move to Ephesus. Later it will move to Alexandria, then to Rome. Today, I don't think there is any particular center of the church. It has gone to the ends of the earth.

I believe that one of the finest vehicles to get the Gospel to the ends of the earth is radio. Through this mechanical means the church can do what has not been accomplished since the first century when the Gospel did penetrate to all the known world.

PHILIP AND THE ETHIOPIAN

In chapters 8, 9, and 10 we find the record of three remarkable instances of conversion. I think that these three have been lifted out and given to us particularly for a lesson. Chapter 8 gives the conversion of the Ethiopian eunuch, a son of Ham. Chapter 9 gives the conversion of Saul of Tarsus, a son of Shem. Chapter 10 gives the conversion of Cornelius, a Roman centurion, a son of Japheth. You will recall that the entire human family is divided into these three categories. This was an ethnological and a geographical division made after the Flood. Ham, Shem, and Japheth were the sons of Noah. We find here that the Gospel reaches out to representatives of these three divisions of the human family.

You will also notice from these examples that in a conversion three factors must be brought into focus before there can be a conversion. All three of these are evident in these three representative conversions.

1. *The work of the Holy Spirit*. The Holy Spirit had taken this man Philip to Samaria where there had been a great moving of the Spirit of God. Then the Holy Spirit moved him down to Gaza, and again we see His loving in the heart of the Ethiopian eunuch. The Spirit of God had gone ahead to prepare the heart and also to prepare the messenger. This leading of the Spirit of God is absolutely essential. I'm afraid that a great deal of personal work is done in a haphazard manner and without the leading of the Spirit of God. I believe that we ought to make it a matter of definite prayer before we talk to anyone. We should talk to the

Lord about the individual before we talk to the individual about the
Lord. It is not simply that we need the Holy Spirit to lead us. What we
need is for the Spirit of God to go ahead of us and prepare the way, then
to call us up to where He is. We want to go where the Spirit of God is
moving. This is the first essential in a conversion. We find it true in the
conversion of the Ethiopian eunuch and also in the conversion of Saul
and of Cornelius.

2. *The Word of God.* "So then faith cometh by hearing, and hearing by the word of God" (Rom. 10:17). The Word of God is the second
essential. The Holy Spirit will take the things of Christ and will reveal
them to an individual. It is the Spirit of God using the Word of God.
But, wait a minute, there must be a human instrument.

3. *The man of God.* The Spirit of God uses the man of God who
delivers the Word of God to produce a son of God, one who is born
again. We will see this in the record of the conversion of this Ethiopian
eunuch.

The second part of chapter 8 brings us to another part of the ministry of Philip. The Gospel had gone to Samaria, and there were many
genuine believers. But we also saw that in Samaria evil came into the
church in the person of Simon the sorcerer. Now, in contrast to Simon
the sorcerer, we come to the experience of Philip with a eunuch from
Ethiopia. Philip led this man to Christ, and he became a genuine believer, a wonderful man of God.

**And the angel of the Lord spake unto Philip, saying,
Arise, and go toward the south unto the way that goeth
down from Jerusalem unto Gaza, which is desert [Acts
8:26].**

Samaria is an area which lies north of Jerusalem. Now Philip is told to
go way down to the south. What we know as the Gaza strip is south,
over along the Mediterranean. This was the trade route down into
Egypt and Ethiopia. He would probably travel through Jerusalem to
get there.

Philip had been speaking to multitudes in Samaria, and now he is
sent down to a desert. He is to leave the place where there has been a

great moving of the Spirit of God and go into a place, a desert, where
there is nobody. However, when he gets there, he finds that God does
have someone to whom he is to witness.

> **And he arose and went: and, behold, a man of Ethiopia,
> an eunuch of great authority under Candace queen of
> the Ethiopians, who had the charge of all her treasure,
> and had come to Jerusalem for to worship,**
>
> **Was returning, and sitting in his chariot read Esaias the
> prophet [Acts 8:27–28].**

We read here that this man of Ethiopia had charge of all the treasure of
the queen. He was actually the Secretary of the Treasury. He was an
official, and a high official of that day. This man was not traveling
alone. He had a great retinue of servants and minor officials with him.
He wasn't sitting in a chariot with the reins in one hand and a book in
the other hand as we see him pictured. This man was sitting back in a
chariot, protected from the sun by a canopy. He had a private chauffeur
and was riding in style.

He was a citizen of Ethiopia, but he had come to Jerusalem to worship. This indicates that he was a proselyte to Judaism. He had just
been to Jerusalem, the center of the Jewish religion. Although Judaism
was the God-given religion, he was leaving the city still in the dark. He
was reading the prophet Isaiah, but he was not understanding what he
was reading.

> **Then the Spirit said unto Philip, Go near, and join thy-
> self to this chariot [Acts 8:29].**

The Holy Spirit is leading, as He must in any conversion. Philip is the
man of God whom the Spirit of God is using. The Word of God is already in that chariot, for the Ethiopian is reading from the prophet
Isaiah.

> **And Philip ran thither to him, and heard him read the
> prophet Esaias, and said, Understandest thou what thou
> readest? [Acts 8:30].**

Philip is a hitchhiker. When he hears what the man is reading, he asks, "Do you understand what you are reading there?" The Ethiopian doesn't; so he stops his retinue and invites Philip to come up and ride with him.

> **And he said, How can I, except some man should guide me? And he desired Philip that he would come up and sit with him.**

> **The place of the scripture which he read was this, He was led as a sheep to the slaughter; and like a lamb dumb before his shearer, so opened he not his mouth:**

> **In his humiliation his judgment was taken away: and who shall declare his generation? for his life is taken from the earth [Acts 8:31–33].**

Where was he reading? You will recognize that this is from the fifty-third chapter of Isaiah. He was reading the seventh and eighth verses. It is obvious that he must have been reading for some time. So it is also obvious that he must have read the preceding verses: "He is despised and rejected of men; a man of sorrows, and acquainted with grief: and we hid as it were our faces from him; he was despised, and we esteemed him not. Surely he hath borne our griefs, and carried our sorrows: yet we did esteem him stricken, smitten of God, and afflicted. But he was wounded for our transgressions, he was bruised for our iniquities: the chastisement of our peace was upon him; and with his stripes we are healed. All we like sheep have gone astray; we have turned every one to his own way; and the Lord hath laid on him the iniquity of us all" (Isa. 53:3–6).

> **And the eunuch answered Philip, and said, I pray thee, of whom speaketh the prophet this? of himself, or of some other man? [Acts 8:34].**

What a marvelous place to begin! When the Spirit of God leads, how wonderfully everything opens up! He will take the things of Christ and make them clear.

> **Then Philip opened his mouth, and began at the same scripture, and preached unto him Jesus [Acts 8:35].**

The Holy Spirit will use the Word of God.

I do not believe that people can be converted by hearing a song. The song may affect a person emotionally and influence the will to make a decision for Christ. However, if the Word of God is not in it, there can be no true conversion. It requires the Word of God. How important that is!

Simon Peter, whom God used so wonderfully in the conversion of multitudes, makes it very clear that the Word of God must be involved if a person is saved. He wrote in his first epistle: "Being born again, not of corruptible seed, but of incorruptible, by the word of God, which liveth and abideth for ever. For all flesh is as grass, and all the glory of man as the flower of grass. The grass withereth, and the flower thereof falleth away: But the word of the Lord endureth for ever. And this is the word which by the gospel is preached unto you" (1 Pet. 1:23–25).

When the Spirit of God uses the Word of God, what is going to happen? These men were in the chariot, discussing the Word of God. Philip was telling the eunuch about Jesus.

> **And as they went on their way, they came unto a certain water: and the eunuch said, See, here is water; what doth hinder me to be baptized?**
>
> **And Philip said, If thou believest with all thine heart, thou mayest. And he answered and said, I believe that Jesus Christ is the Son of God [Acts 8:36–37].**

Remember that Philip had had an experience with Simon the sorcerer up there in Samaria. He is not about to have a repetition of that. When this man asks for water baptism, Philip wants to be very sure that he believes with all his heart.

> **And he commanded the chariot to stand still: and they went down both into the water, both Philip and the eunuch; and he baptized him.**

> And when they were come up out of the water, the Spirit
> of the Lord caught away Philip, that the eunuch saw him
> no more: and he went on his way rejoicing [Acts
> 8:38–39].

Philip is snatched off the page of Scripture. He is not needed here anymore. The Ethiopian rides off the pages of Scripture in his chariot. He went on his way, rejoicing. Now what about this man? The first great church was not in the United States, nor was it in Europe, nor was it in Jerusalem, nor was it in Asia Minor. The first great church was in northern Africa. The Ethiopian evidently went back and through his witness and his influence, a church was begun there. You would find it very profitable to read about the early church in North Africa.

Now what about Philip?

> But Philip was found at Azotus: and passing through he
> preached in all the cities, till he came to Caesarea [Acts
> 8:40].

Azotus is Ashdod, which is over in the Gaza strip. To reach Caesarea, he would have gone through Joppa. Tel Aviv is there today. So he went, preaching the Gospel along the coast up to Caesarea. The Gospel has gone to Judea and to Samaria and is moving out. The eunuch has carried it down to Ethiopia. Philip is carrying it along the coast to Caesarea.

CHAPTER 9

This chapter tells about another remarkable conversion. The conversion of the Ethiopian eunuch was in a chariot; the conversion of Saul of Tarsus was down in the dust. Probably he was riding a little donkey when he went up to Damascus, and he was knocked right down into the dust.

When we get to the Book of Philippians, we shall look at the theological, psychological, and philosophical aspects of the conversion of Saul of Tarsus. Here, we are dealing with the facts of what actually happened on the road to Damascus.

THE CONVERSION OF SAUL OF TARSUS

And Saul, yet breathing out threatenings and slaughter against the disciples of the Lord, went unto the high priest.

And desired of him letters to Damascus to the synagogues, that if he found any of this way, whether they were men or women, he might bring them bound unto Jerusalem [Acts 9:1–2].

When the persecution broke out in Jerusalem, the church went underground. The apostles remained in Jerusalem, but many of the others were scattered—we found Philip up in Samaria and along the Mediterranean coast. The thing that triggered it was the stoning of Stephen, followed by persecution.

The other religious leaders in Jerusalem were satisfied after they had run the Christians out of Jerusalem. They were willing to let it stay at that point. But not Saul of Tarsus! He was the one who was breathing out threatenings and slaughter. He hated Jesus Christ. I do not think that the Lord Jesus Christ ever has had an enemy greater than this man Saul of Tarsus. He went to the high priest and said, "Look, I've heard that a group of them have run off up there to Damascus, and I'm going after them." The fact of the matter is that he intended to ferret them out, anywhere they went. His goal was to exterminate the Christians.

> **And as he journeyed, he came near Damascus: and suddenly there shined round about him a light from heaven:**
>
> **And he fell to the earth, and heard a voice saying unto him, Saul, Saul, why persecutest thou me? [Acts 9:3–4].**

Paul will recount this incident twice more in the Book of Acts. In fact, Paul never tired of telling about his conversion. We find him going over it again in his Epistle to the Philippians where he gets right down to the heart of the matter and tells what really happened to him. Here we are simply given the facts. He will go over them again when he gives his testimony before king Agrippa—that is a masterpiece.

> **And he said, Who art thou, Lord? And the Lord said, I am Jesus whom thou persecutest: it is hard for thee to kick against the pricks [Acts 9:5].**

Will you notice, here, the ignorance of Saul? He was possibly the most brilliant man of his day. He was probably a graduate of the University of Tarsus, the greatest Greek university of that day. He was a student in the school of Gamaliel, the Hebrew scholar. He was trained in the details of the Jewish religion. But he did not know the Lord Jesus Christ. "Who art thou, Lord?" Friend, to know *Him* is life. Saul didn't know Him!

> **And he trembling and astonished said, Lord, what wilt thou have me to do? And the Lord said unto him, Arise, and go into the city, and it shall be told thee what thou must do [Acts 9:6].**

Saul is right down in the dust on that road to Damascus. This is a remarkable conversion. He immediately reveals his conversion. This man who hated the Lord Jesus, who did everything he could against Him, now calls Him "Lord." And he asks what the Lord would have him do. He is ready to do the bidding of the Lord. He has been completely changed. "Wherefore by their fruits ye shall know them" (Matt. 7:20). We can surely tell what has happened to this man.

> **And the men which journeyed with him stood speechless, hearing a voice, but seeing no man [Acts 9:7].**

Later on it says that they didn't hear. Is this a conflict? No, they heard a voice but that was all. They couldn't understand what was said. It didn't make any sense to them. They didn't see anyone. There was no one for them to see. They were speechless with amazement. We shall see this is more detail in Acts 22 and 26.

> **And Saul arose from the earth; and when his eyes were opened, he saw no man: but they led him by the hand, and brought him into Damascus.**
>
> **And he was three days without sight, and neither did eat nor drink [Acts 9:8–9].**

This man was blinded by the light that he had seen from heaven. Here was a man who was puzzled as much as any man has ever been. Some people jump up and down when they are converted. Some shout for joy. Not Saul of Tarsus. There never was a man as confused as he was. Had we met him on one of those three days in Damascus and had we asked him what had happened to him, his answer would have been, "I don't know." But he is going to find out.

> **And there was a certain disciple at Damascus, named Ananias; and to him said the Lord in a vision, Ananias. And he said, Behold, I am here, Lord.**
>
> **And the Lord said unto him, Arise, and go into the**

> street which is called Straight, and inquire in the house
> of Judas for one called Saul, of Tarsus: for, behold, he
> prayeth,
>
> And hath seen in a vision a man named Ananias com-
> ing in, and putting his hand on him, that he might re-
> ceive his sight [Acts 9:10–12].

Saul of Tarsus, a brilliant young man, is sitting in darkness and confusion. The Spirit of God comes to another man, Ananias, and sends him
over to Saul of Tarsus.

> Then Ananias answered, Lord, I have heard by many of
> this man, how much evil he hath done to thy saints at
> Jerusalem:
>
> And here he hath authority from the chief priests to bind
> all that call on thy name.
>
> But the Lord said unto him, Go thy way: for he is a cho-
> sen vessel unto me, to bear my name before the Gentiles,
> and kings, and the children of Israel:
>
> For I will shew him how great things he must suffer for
> my name's sake [Acts 9:13–16].

God states two reasons for calling Saul. He was God's chosen vessel for
two things. First, he was to bear the name of Jesus. Notice that he is not
called a *witness* as the disciples were. Although Paul may have seen
Jesus at His crucifixion, he had not walked with Him in the days of His
flesh. He really knew nothing about Him until that day on the road to
Damascus. Now he is to bear that name. That is the same name we are
to bear today, the name of Jesus.

He is to bear that name before three different groups: Gentiles,
kings, and the children of Israel. Gentiles are first on the list. Paul will
be the great Apostle to the Gentiles. Then to kings—he will appear
before kings, probably including Nero himself, and then to the nation
Israel. When Paul goes into a city, he always will begin in the Jewish

synagogue. The synagogue will be his springboard to put him into the community, into the life of the city. From there he will reach the Gentiles. But he will go to the Jews first.

Second, the Lord said He will show Saul what great things he must suffer for His name's sake. He is chosen to suffer for Jesus Christ. In my judgment, there has never been anyone else who has suffered for the Lord as Paul the apostle suffered. None of us dare say, "I'm suffering more than anyone else. Why does God let this happen to me?" We may be suffering, or we may think we are suffering more than we are. At any rate, none of us suffer as Paul the apostle suffered for the Lord.

Now as we look back on this remarkable conversion, you may remember that I said conversion requires the Holy Spirit using the Word of God through a man of God. Does this prove true in the conversion of Saul of Tarsus?

The Lord Jesus appeared to Saul personally. Before the Lord Jesus left His disciples, He told them that He was going away but that He would not leave them orphans. He promised them that He would send His Holy Spirit, and this is what the Spirit would do: "He shall glorify me: for he shall receive of mine, and shall shew it unto you. All things that the Father hath are mine: therefore said I, that he shall take of mine, and shall shew it unto you" (John 16:14–15). Now I think that when our resurrected Lord appeared to Saul personally, the Spirit of God opened his eyes spiritually and closed them physically so that he might see the Lord Jesus. So the Holy Spirit was definitely at work.

How about the Word of God? How was that used in the conversion of Paul? Saul of Tarsus was a Pharisee. He knew a great deal about the Word of God. In fact, if there ever has been anyone saturated with the Word of God, he was Saul of Tarsus. When reading his epistles, it becomes obvious that he was very familiar with the Old Testament. The Holy Spirit and the Word of God were operative in Saul's conversion.

How can one say that God used a man of God as the human instrument to reach Saul? Although a man of God was not present at the time, I believe the man whom the Lord used to reach Saul was none other than Stephen. These two young men, Saul and Stephen, met only once, and that was when Saul stood with those who killed him. Stephen had looked up into the heavens and said, "I see heaven open and Jesus standing there!" (see Acts 7:56). Saul of Tarsus looked up into the heavens and couldn't see anything. Then he looked into the face of Stephen, and he knew that Stephen was actually seeing something. I believe that Saul actually hoped that the heavens would open and that he, too, could have a vision of God. And he did on the Damascus road. It was Jesus Christ who was revealed to him.

I believe that God uses a human instrument in the conversion of every individual although that individual may not be present at the moment of the conversion. That is the reason you and I should cast our influence for the Lord Jesus Christ at all times.

Recently I received a letter from a man who is a barber. A certain man had been his customer for twenty years. One time when the customer got out of the chair and was paying for his haircut, he asked the barber, "Have you ever heard Dr. McGee on the radio?" The barber said he had not; so the customer walked over to his radio and turned it to the station on which we can be heard in that town. He said, "Every morning at eight o'clock! You listen to him!" That was the last time these two men saw each other. The customer died suddenly within a day or so. You can guess the end of the story. The barber started listening to the program. He had been listening to it for over two years when he wrote to me. He has come to know Jesus Christ as his Savior. The human instrument in his conversion was his old customer.

Dr. C. I. Scofield is the man who edited the Scofield Bible. Before his conversion he was an outstanding international lawyer, but he had the problem of being a very heavy drinker. He had a godly mother who prayed for him continually. She died before Dr. Scofield was converted. On one occasion Dr. Lewis Sperry Chafer was praying with Dr. Scofield. He told us that he heard Dr. Scofield say, "Lord, if my mother doesn't know that I have been converted, would You please tell her so?" God uses a human instrument in the conversion of every person although that person may not be present at the moment of conversion. I don't think a person can be converted without a human instrument. So why don't you be an instrument? That doesn't mean you have to get a person to his knees; it does mean that you get the good news of Jesus Christ to him. There will not be a real conversion without a man of God using the Word of God, directed by the Spirit of God.

Now, going back to Saul of Tarsus where we left him in Damascus, he is still sitting in solitary blindness, praying. Brilliant young man that he is, he is still somewhat confused since his conversion. So the Spirit of God appeared to Ananias and sent him over to help him.

And Ananias went his way, and entered into the house; and putting his hands on him said, Brother Saul, the Lord, even Jesus, that appeared unto thee in the way as thou camest, hath sent me, that thou mightest receive thy sight, and be filled with the Holy Ghost [Acts 9:17].

What a change! He is still Saul of Tarsus, but now he is *Brother* Saul. He is not the enemy. He is a brother. Any person who loves the Lord Jesus Christ is a brother to any other believer. Unfortunately, I must add that brothers don't always act like brothers.

Saul is to receive his physical sight. Also, he is to be filled with the Holy Spirit. He is to be filled with the Holy Spirit for service. This is the experience which reveals itself in the life of the believer. He was baptized with the Holy Spirit on the Damascus road. In other words, he was saved on the Damascus road. But it wasn't until this man Ananias came to him that he was filled with the Holy Spirit. He is going to become a witness for the Lord Jesus. He will receive his physical weight and his spiritual sight.

And immediately there fell from his eyes as it had been scales: and he received sight forthwith, and arose, and was baptized [Acts 9:18].

Now he is baptized with water as a sign and seal of his conversion. The water had nothing to do with his salvation. He had been baptized by the Holy Spirit—that is, he had been saved on the Damascus road. When Ananias had laid his hands on him, he had been filled with the Holy Spirit for service. And now he is baptized with water.

And when he had received meat, he was strengthened, Then was Saul certain days with the disciples which were at Damascus [Acts 9:19].

SAUL BEGINS TO WITNESS AT DAMASCUS

**And straightway he preached Christ in the synagogues,
that he is the Son of God [Acts 9:20].**

Saul of Tarsus begins to witness immediately. Why? Because he is
filled with the Holy Spirit. He began to preach "Christ in the synagogues, that he is the Son of God."

Friend, you must know who Christ is before you can believe what
He did. He died to pay the penalty for your sins. It is because He is the
Son of God that He could die for your sins. I couldn't die for your sins;
you couldn't die for mine. No human being can die a redemptive death
for another human being. Only Christ could do this because He is the
Son of God. So Saul began to preach that Christ is the Son of God. That
is the first thing you must know.

**But all that heard him were amazed, and said; Is not
this he that destroyed them which called on this name
in Jerusalem, and came hither for that intent, that he
might bring them bound unto the chief priests?**

**But Saul increased the more in strength, and con-
founded the Jews which dwelt in Damascus, proving
that this is very Christ [Acts 9:21–22].**

The "very Christ" means the very *Messiah*. Saul confounded the Jews
by preaching this. Saul of Tarsus is number one in several depart-
ments. He is number one in suffering; he is number one as a missionary. I think he is also number one in his I.Q.—he was a brilliant man.
He was able to confound those who attempted to tackle him intellectu-
ally.

**And after that many days were fulfilled, the Jews took
counsel to kill him:**

**But their laying await was known of Saul. And they
watched the gates day and night to kill him.**

> Then the disciples took him by night, and let him down
> by the wall in a basket [Acts 9:23-25].

When the Jews couldn't win by argument, they resorted to another tactic, which was to eliminate the enemy.

I'm sure it must have been quite a thrilling experience to have been let down over the wall in a basket. Yet we never read anywhere in the New Testament that Paul toured the Roman Empire giving a lecture on the subject, "Over the Wall in a Basket." That ought to be a lesson for a great many folk who deal in sensationalism today. Here is a man who has had a most remarkable experience, but he has something more important to present.

We must never let out *experience* get in the way of presenting Christ. We must never let our *person* get in the way of the Person of Christ. Sometimes I hear the very pious prayer, "Hide the preacher behind the cross." No, friend, that is not what he needs. Rather, we should pray, "Help the preacher to present Christ in such a way that the Spirit of God can take the things of Christ and show them to us. Help him to present Christ!" This was Paul's method.

SAUL IN JERUSALEM

> And when Saul was come to Jerusalem, he assayed to
> join himself to the disciples: but they were all afraid of
> him, and believed not that he was a disciple [Acts 9:26].

They thought this was a deception on the part of Saul of Tarsus, that he was worming his way in. They were experiencing persecution. And they probably had heard of Simon the sorcerer and the tactics he used in Samaria.

> But Barnabas took him, and brought him to the apostles, and declared unto them how he had seen the Lord
> in the way, and that he had spoken to him, and how he
> had preached boldly at Damascus in the name of Jesus
> [Acts 9:27].

Good old Barnabas, whose very name means the "son of consolation and comfort"! He comes over and puts his arms around Saul. What a blessing he was to him! How we still need people who will put their arms around some new Christian and will help that new Christian along. Barnabas becomes the sponsor of Saul.

And he was with them coming in and going out at Jerusalem [Acts 9:28].

Paul is accepted into the assembly at Jerusalem and joins forces with the Jerusalem church.

And he spake boldly in the name of the Lord Jesus, and disputed against the Grecians: but they went about to slay him [Acts 9:29].

These are not Greeks. They are Israelites who have a Greek background. They had been brought up outside Israel somewhere in the Greek world. The witness of Saul was so powerful that they concluded the only way to get rid of his effectiveness was to eliminate him, to kill him.

Which when the brethren knew, they brought him down to Caesarea, and sent him forth to Tarsus [Acts 9:30].

Paul goes to his hometown. He probably went back home to tell his father and mother, brothers and sisters, and other relatives about Christ. We know nothing about them. Paul never talked about his family—with one exception. In Romans 16 he mentions some folk who are related to him.

Then had the churches rest throughout all Judaea and Galilee and Samaria, and were edified; and walking in the fear of the Lord, and in the comfort of the Holy Ghost, were multiplied [Acts 9:31].

The church continued to grow. The Gospel went into Judea, Galilee, and Samaria. It will start to go to the ends of the earth very shortly.

PETER'S MINISTRY IN LYDDA AND JOPPA

And it came to pass, as Peter passed throughout all quarters, he came down also to the saints which dwelt at Lydda.

And there he found a certain man named Aeneas, which had kept his bed eight years, and was sick of the palsy.

And Peter said unto him, Aeneas, Jesus Christ maketh thee whole: arise, and make thy bed. And he arose immediately.

And all that dwelt at Lydda and Saron saw him, and turned to the Lord [Acts 9:32–35].

Because Peter was an apostle, he had the sign gifts of an apostle.

Now there was at Joppa a certain disciple named Tabitha, which by interpretation is called Dorcas: this woman was full of good works, and almsdeeds which she did [Acts 9:36].

This woman was engaged in social service. She had the gift of sewing. Do you mean to tell me that sewing is a gift of the Holy Spirit? Yes, it was for this woman. Many people today are seeking for some exciting, fleshly gift such as speaking in tongues. May I suggest seeking a gift that is practical? I say very carefully and kindly, "Dear sister, learn to sew."

Sewing was a gift of Dorcas. I doubt that she ever spoke at a missionary meeting or taught a women's Bible class. I don't think she ever had such an opportunity because she was one of the early saints. But she did a lot of wonderful things for folk.

And it came to pass in those days, that she was sick, and died: whom when they had washed, they laid her in an upper chamber [Acts 9:37].

Notice how the Christians prepared for burial in that day.

And forasmuch as Lydda was nigh to Joppa, and the disciples had heard that Peter was there, they sent unto him two men, desiring him that he would not delay to come to them [Acts 9:38].

They sent word from Joppa to Lydda that a very wonderful woman in the church there in Joppa had died. They apparently believed that Simon Peter could raise her from the dead. At least they asked him to come down.

Then Peter arose and went with them. When he was come, they brought him into the upper chamber: and all the widows stood by him weeping, and shewing the coats and garments which Dorcas made, while she was with them [Acts 9:39].

You will notice that it was the widows who conducted this fashion show. They were all showing off the garments that Dorcas had made. Why did the widows do it? Because they were poor. They wouldn't have had any clothes if it had not been for Dorcas. She had sewn their clothes for them. This was her ministry. Sewing was her gift of the Holy Spirit.

But Peter put them all forth, and kneeled down, and prayed; and turning him to the body said, Tabitha, arise. And she opened her eyes: and when she saw Peter, she sat up.

And he gave her his hand, and lifted her up, and when he had called the saints and widows, presented her alive [Acts 9:40–41].

Here is an example of the exercise of a sign gift. We have in the Book of Acts, the historical book of the church, the ministries of Simon Peter who was an apostle and of Paul who was an apostle. Simon Peter was a minister to his own people; yet he was the one to open the door for the Gentiles. Saul of Tarsus became the apostle Paul, and he was the Apostle to the Gentiles. The record states that each one raised a person from the dead. Quite possibly they raised others, but these are recorded to show that these men had sign gifts. They could perform miracles. They could heal the sick. They could raise the dead. These were the marks, the evidences of an apostle. They were apostolic gifts. Paul says that the apostles are the foundation of the church in the sense that the church is built on them. They are the ones who put down the New Testament on which the church is actually built.

Today we do not need sign gifts. The issue today is doctrine. At the end of the era of New Testament writings, the apostle John wrote his epistles. Listen to his instructions for detecting deceivers: "If there come any unto you, and bring not this doctrine, receive him not into your house, neither bid him God speed: For he that biddeth him God speed is partaker of his evil deeds" (2 John 10–11).

Toward the end of Paul's own ministry the record clearly shows that Paul did not exercise the gift of healing. For instance, notice that he left Trophimus at Miletum sick (2 Tim. 4:20). Why did not Paul heal his friend Trophimus? Paul, you see, had come to the end of his ministry, and the sign gifts even then were beginning to disappear from the church. At the beginning of Paul's ministry nothing of the New Testament had been written. Paul himself wrote the second book of the New Testament. When he went into a new territory with his message, what was his authority? He had no authority except sign gifts. However, after the New Testament was in written form, the emphasis shifted from sign gifts to correct doctrine. Paul warns that if a man does not have correct doctrine—even if he is an angel from heaven—you should not receive him. "But though we, or an angel from heaven, preach any other gospel unto you than that which we have preached unto you, let him be accursed" (Gal. 1:8).

However, in the early days of the church, the apostles' sign gifts were important. Notice the reaction of those who heard of Dorcas being restored to life.

And it was known throughout all Joppa; and many believed in the Lord [Acts 9:42].

The sign gifts were used to confirm to them the Gospel of grace.

And it came to pass, that he tarried many days in Joppa with one Simon a tanner [Acts 9:43].

A tanner used acid to tan his animal hides. It really made the place quite odoriferous. When I was in Joppa, we were shown the place where Simon Peter is said to have stayed. Joppa is a rather picturesque village right on the water's edge, and the tanner's house was down there. The house looks old enough to have been there that long. So this may well have been the place where Simon Peter stayed.

CHAPTER 10

THEME: Conversion of Cornelius, the Roman centurion (son of Japheth)

Chapter 10 continues the record of the ministry of Simon Peter. Later Peter will pass from the scene, and the history will continue with the ministry of the apostle Paul. Although Paul is the Apostle to the Gentiles, Peter opened the door to the Gentiles by entering the home of Cornelius and presenting salvation through Christ to his household.

CORNELIUS' VISION

There was a certain man in Caesarea called Cornelius, a centurion of the band called the Italian band [Acts 10:1].

Remember that Paul had been in Caesarea (Acts 9:30) and probably some of the other apostles had been preaching the Gospel along the coast. Tel Aviv is really a part of old Joppa. As one travels up the coast from Joppa, the next place of any size is Caesarea, which was really a Roman city. It was the place where Pilate lived. The governor and those who ruled the land stayed there. This is where Cornelius was stationed. He was a centurion, which means he was a commander of a hundred soldiers in the Roman army. The Italian band was a cohort of Roman soldiers recruited in Italy.

A devout man, and one that feared God with all his house, which gave much alms to the people, and prayed to God alway [Acts 10:2].

He was "a devout man." That means his worship was rightly directed. He recognized his dependence upon that which is divine. Remember that even a pagan can have devotion and a deep conviction to his gods. Sometimes we wish that Christians today had more devotion and conviction.

He was a devout man and "one that feared God." He was not a Jewish proselyte in the strict sense of the term, but gravitated toward Judaism and could be called a "proselyte of the Gate." Today we might say that he was a man who lived in the neighborhood, attended church on special occasions, was friendly toward the church, but was not actually a Christian. That could have been Cornelius. He feared God.

He "gave much alms to the people" means he gave many gifts of charity to the Jewish people. The nation Israel has always laid great stress upon giving. God had taught them this in the Old Testament. We speak of the tithe, but it is obvious from the Mosaic system that they actually gave three tenths. They gave for the running of the government (which was a theocracy at the beginning), they gave for the maintenance of the temple, and they gave a tenth of all that they produced. So they have been a giving, generous people.

It is interesting that even today many of our eleemosynary, that is, charitable foundations, were established by Jews. There is no group of people in our day that gives as generously as does the Jewish community in its support of the nation Israel. They are a very generous people.

Cornelius "prayed to God always." This centurion took his needs to God. He needed to have more light. He wanted it. He probably didn't really know too much about prayer, but he prayed.

He saw in a vision evidently about the ninth hour of the day an angel of God coming in to him, and saying unto him, Cornelius [Acts 10:3].

This centurion was an officer in the Roman army, a career officer, and a man of influence. Also he had a tremendous influence in his own household, as we shall see. He was a good man to all outward observation. In America today he would pass for a Christian, a Christian of the highest degree, an outstanding man. But he actually was not a Christian. He had not even heard the Gospel.

He is an example of a man who lived up to the light which he had. John 1:9 says this of Jesus: "That was the true Light, which lighteth every man that cometh into the world." This centurion had not met Jesus Christ nor come into His presence, but he was living up to the light that he had. Paul is referring to those who do not live by the light they have in Romans 1:19–20: "Because that which may be known of God is manifest in them; for God hath shewed it unto them. For the invisible things of him from the creation of the world are clearly seen, being understood by the things that are made, even his eternal power and Godhead; so that they are without excuse." This is God's answer to that oft-repeated question, "What about the poor pagan, that 'good' heathen, who wants to know God but never had a chance? Is he lost?" The answer is that God will get light to such a person. God will enable him to hear the Gospel. Now how will God get the Gospel to Cornelius? The barriers seem insurmountable. The church at this time—and for the first eight years—was exclusively Jewish.

These Christian Jews were still going to the temple and observing many Jewish customs. They could do that under grace because they were trusting Christ. Then the Gospel broke over into Samaria. The Jews in Jerusalem were surprised, but they recognized the hand of God in this. Now how is God going to open the door of the Gospel to the Gentiles? God used perhaps the most prejudiced and religious bigot, the greatest extremist of the day. Obviously, the Holy Spirit directed every move in getting the Gospel to the Gentiles. My friend, all genuine Christian work is directed by the Holy Spirit. No other work amounts to anything. The Holy Spirit had to work in the heart of the Gentile; the Holy Spirit had to work in the heart of the Jew. The Holy Spirit directed the bringing of the Gospel to the Gentile world.

And when he looked on him, he was afraid, and said, What is it, Lord? And he said unto him, Thy prayers and thine alms are come up for a memorial before God [Acts 10:4].

An angel of God appeared to Cornelius in a vision. He was not dreaming but was given this vision while he was praying.

Now I do want you to notice that there are certain things that do count before God. These are things which can in no way merit salvation, but they are things which God notes. The prayers of Cornelius and his alms had come up for a memorial before God, and God brought the Gospel to him. Wherever there is a man who seeks after God as Cornelius did, that man is going to hear the Gospel of the grace of God. God will see that he gets it.

> **And now send men to Joppa, and call for one Simon, whose surname is Peter:**
>
> **He lodgeth with one Simon a tanner, whose house is by the sea side: he shall tell thee what thou oughtest to do [Acts 10:5-6].**

The angel tells him where to find Peter. He doesn't need more of an address. The odor of those hides down in that vat will lead them to the right place!

> **And when the angel which spake unto Cornelius was departed, he called two of his household servants, and a devout soldier of them that waited on him continually;**
>
> **And when he had declared all these things unto them, he sent them to Joppa [Acts 10:7-8].**

These men won't have any trouble finding the tanner's house. While they are on their way, God must prepare Simon Peter.

PETER'S VISION

> **On the morrow, as they went on their journey, and drew nigh unto the city, Peter went up upon the housetop to pray about the sixth hour [Acts 10:9].**

It is absolutely necessary for God to prepare Simon Peter. You see, Simon Peter didn't have the breadth that Paul had. Although he didn't have the background or the training that Paul had, God can use him differently. I believe it is a tremendous mistake to think that every person has to be poured into the same mold for God to use him.

> **And he became very hungry, and would have eaten: but while they made ready, he fell into a trance.**
>
> **And saw heaven opened, and a certain vessel descending unto him, as it had been a great sheet knit at the four corners, and let down to the earth:**
>
> **Wherein were al manner of fourfooted beasts of the earth, and wild beasts, and creeping things, and fowls of the air [Acts 10:10–12].**

Notice that there were beasts, all kinds of birds, and all kinds of bugs.

> **And there came a voice to him, Rise, Peter; kill, and eat.**
>
> **But Peter said, Not so, Lord; for I have never eaten any thing that is common or unclean [Acts 10:13–14].**

While Peter is wondering what this means, a voice speaks to him. Isn't it interesting that he calls Him, "Lord," but he doesn't obey what the Lord tells him to do?

Now don't miss this. Here is a man who is on this side of the Day of Pentecost. He is living in this age of grace when it makes no difference whether we eat meat or whether we don't eat meat. However, Peter is still abiding by the Mosaic system, and he is not eating anything that is ceremonially unclean. He is sincere and honest about it. Someone may say that he ought to be broad-minded and eat everything. Well, you see that the Lord is teaching him that he is no longer under the Mosaic system and is free to eat anything. Today the big problem is that some people decide they don't want to eat meat and then they try to put everyone else under that same system. My friend, under grace you can eat meat or not eat meat. That is your business. Eating some certain food may give you indigestion, but it certainly will not change your relationship with the Lord.

> And the voice spake unto him again the second time,
> What God hath cleansed, that call not thou common
> [Acts 10:15].

What God has made clean, don't you call unclean. You can eat anything because God has said so.

> This was done thrice: and the vessel was received up
> again into heaven [Acts 10:16].

Peter was left wondering what it was all about.

> Now while Peter doubted in himself what this vision
> which he had seen should mean, behold, the men which
> were sent from Cornelius had made inquiry for Simon's
> house, and stood before the gate.
>
> And called, and asked whether Simon, which was surnamed Peter, were lodged there.
>
> While Peter thought on the vision, the Spirit said unto
> him, Behold, three men seek thee.
>
> Arise therefore, and get thee down, and go with them,
> doubting nothing: for I have sent them.
>
> Then Peter went down to the men which were sent unto
> him from Cornelius; and said, Behold, I am he whom ye
> seek: what is the cause wherefore ye are come?
>
> And they said, Cornelius the centurion, a just man, and
> one that feareth God, and of good report among all the
> nation of the Jews, was warned from God by an holy
> angel to send for thee into his house, and to hear words
> of thee [Acts 10:17–22].

Simon Peter is go to Caesarea. This little delegation from Cornelius gives an explanation to him, then extends an invitation to come with them to the house of Cornelius.

THE CONVERSION OF CORNELIUS

Then called he them in, and lodged them. And on the morrow Peter went away with them, and certain brethren from Joppa accompanied him.

And the morrow after they entered into Caesarea. And Cornelius waited for them, and had called together his kinsmen and near friends.

And as Peter was coming in, Cornelius met him, and fell down at his feet, and worshipped him [Acts 10:23–25].

We can see that Cornelius had quite an influence on his family and friends. He has called them together for this occasion. Also we can see that Cornelius is still a pagan, a heathen. When he is instructed by an angel to send for Simon Peter, he concludes that this man must really be important; so he falls down and worships Peter.

It is interesting to see Simon Peter's reaction to this. Friend, Simon Peter would never have let you get down to kiss his big toe. He just wouldn't permit it.

But Peter took him up, saying, Stand up; I myself also am a man [Acts 10:26].

Peter reached down and pulled him to his feet and said, "Stand up; I myself also am a *man*." I like the way he did that.

And as he talked with him, he went in, and found many that were come together.

And he said unto them, Ye know how that it is an unlawful thing for a man that is a Jew to keep company, or come unto one of another nation; but God hath shewed me that I should not call any man common or unclean [Acts 10:27–28].

Peter stepped into the house. What a step that was! It was the first time that Peter had ever been in a gentile house. He still is really a little baffled at God's command to go there.

He violates the first rule of homiletics when he begins his message with an apology. What he says is not a friendly thing to say. In fact, it is an insult. In essence, he said, "If you really want to know how I felt about this, well, I just didn't want to come. I've never been in the home of a Gentile before. Never before have I gone into a place that is unclean!" But he does go on to add, "Even though I have never before been in an unclean home, God has told me not to call any man unclean. We are all sinners and we are all savable." How would you feel, especially if you are a lady who is a housekeeper, if some visitor came into your home and his first words were, "I am coming into your home, which I consider dirty"? You wouldn't exactly respond with a warm, friendly feeling, would you? Yet this is the substance of what Simon Peter said.

Because God had showed him that there was neither clean nor unclean, he continues his message.

> **Therefore came I unto you without gainsaying, as soon as I was sent for: I ask therefore for what intent ye have sent for me? [Acts 10:29].**

This amazes me. Why would Simon Peter ask that question? Why didn't he immediately begin to tell them about Jesus Christ? Well, you see, the Spirit of God is in charge here, and He keeps Peter from rushing right into this.

This should be an important lesson for us. So often we are rather brisk and even crude in our witnessing. Because we find it difficult to witness, generally when we do it, we are very amateurish about it. We do it so abruptly and in such a way that often it offends people.

We need to be led by the Spirit of God. I personally believe that the finest kind of evangelism today is prayer evangelism. I mean that we should begin by praying for an individual. Then the day will come when we need to put legs on the prayer. Ask God to lead you. Friend, I *know* that He will lead you. If you have been praying for a loved one, or a friend, or a stranger, don't just go to him in your own strength and in the power of the flesh. If you do, you will fail. Let God be the One to lead you.

Let me share with you one of my first experiences of witnessing. When I was a student in college, I was very zealous to be a witness for God, but I was rather timid about it, and, very frankly, I wanted to be sure I had the leading of the Holy Spirit. I didn't have any money for bus or train fare, so I did a lot of hitchhiking. One time when I was out on the highway, a man in a brand new Model A Ford drove by and stopped fifty yards past me. Then he motioned for me to come on and get in. He said that he always looked over a hitchhiker before he picked one up. He introduced himself and told me he was a salesman for drug companies. He asked where I was going and I told him it was to Memphis. Well, he was going all the way to Memphis and he would be glad to take me all the way, but he did need to stop at several drug stores on the way to get his orders from them. Obviously, that was fine with me.

As we rode along, we talked of everything under the sun. Under my breath I was praying, "Lord I'd like to witness to this man, but You will have to open the door for me. I'm not going to broach the subject because if I do, he'll think he has some religious nut in the car with him. If I open the door, *he* will probably open the car door and tell me to get out." So we rode along some more and just talked and talked. Finally he asked me whether I'd mind driving for him. Of course, I would love to drive that new car; so I did. He sat there and relaxed.

We got about sixty miles from Memphis and we had run out of conversation. There was a lull, and I was still praying, "Lord, we're getting near Memphis and there still hasn't been a door open for me. I'm not going to open it because I'm afraid he'll throw me out. You open the door for me if You want me to witness." We rode on for about ten more minutes, and then out of a clear sky he said, "You know, my wife and I went to church yesterday." He looked at me and laughed, and I laughed. Then he said, "I don't go very often. But that preacher said the funniest thing. He said Jesus was coming to this earth again. What do you think about that?"

Well, friend, I told him. Then I told him all about the first coming of the Lord Jesus. Finally I said, "The second coming of Christ means nothing to you now. You've got to come to Christ and accept what He did for you the first time He came if you are to have an interest in His second coming." This man was wide open. He drove me to the dormitory where I stayed at the college. He parked there and said, "I want to see you again." So I just blurted out, "Wouldn't you like to accept Christ as your Savior?" He said, "I sure would." I told him he could do that right there in the car. So we bowed our heads in prayer. I prayed and then asked him to pray, and he accepted Christ. Now I'll be honest with you, I would never have opened my mouth if the Lord hadn't prompted him to open up the conversation. We need to be led by the Spirit. The Holy Spirit had prepared his heart, and his conversion was genuine. The first sermon I preached after I was ordained in Nashville, as I looked down at the congregation, I noticed this man and his wife. He just sat there and smiled. Afterward I invited him to join my church. He said they had already joined a good church over in another part of town. He and his wife had become active Christians. What a wonderful experience that was!

We ought to be very careful in our witnessing that we are being led by the Spirit of God. Simon Peter does not walk right in and begin lecturing or preaching. He first finds out what is going on. "Why have you called for me? Why did you send these men for me?"

> **And Cornelius said, Four days ago I was fasting until this hour; and at the ninth hour I prayed in my house, and, behold, a man stood before me in bright clothing.**

> **And said, Cornelius thy prayer is heard, and thine alms are had in remembrance in the sight of God.**

> **Send therefore to Joppa, and call hither Simon, whose surname is Peter; he is lodged in the house of one Simon a tanner by the sea side: who, when he cometh, shall speak unto thee.**

> **Immediately therefore I sent to thee; and thou hast well done that thou art come. Now therefore are we all here present before God, to hear all things that are commanded thee of God [Acts 10:30–33].**

Cornelius tells him, "I really don't know why I sent for you, except God told me to send for Simon Peter. You must have some message for me."

> **Then Peter opened his mouth, and said, Of a truth I perceive that God is no respecter of persons:**
>
> **But in every nation he that feareth him, and worketh righteousness, is accepted with him.**
>
> **The word which God sent unto the children of Israel, preaching peace by Jesus Christ: (he is Lord of all:)**
>
> **That word, I say, ye know, which was published throughout all Judaea, and began from Galilee, after the baptism which John preached [Acts 10:34-37].**

Apparently Cornelius and those assembled with him would have heard certain basic facts about Jesus of Nazareth and also about the ministry of John the Baptist.

> **How God anointed Jesus of Nazareth with the Holy Ghost and with power: who went about doing good, and healing all that were oppressed of the devil; for God was with him.**
>
> **And we are witnesses of all things which he did both in the land of the Jews, and in Jerusalem; whom they slew and hanged on a tree:**
>
> **Him God raised up the third day, and shewed him openly [Acts 10:38-40].**

Notice carefully what Simon Peter does. He presents the facts concerning Jesus Christ, assuming there are some of the incidents which they already know. He makes it very clear to them that this Jesus was crucified on a tree and that He rose again on the third day. God raised Him and showed Him openly. This is the Gospel. Nothing short of that will do.

This past Christmas I received many cards on which were printed the rather well-known message, "One Solitary Life." It is very fine; there is no question about that. It is very readable, but there is a strange omission—a solitary omission in it. The most important fact is not recorded. It records that Jesus died, even mentions that He was buried, but completely leaves out His resurrection. Friend, there is not a single sermon preached, as recorded in the Book of Acts, that does not mention the resurrection of Jesus Christ. That is the very heart of the Gospel. Until that is preached, the Gospel has not been preached. Jesus Christ died, He was buried, He rose again from the dead. Those are the historical facts. Your relationship to a *risen* Savior determines your eternal destiny. He died for our sins according to the Scriptures, and He was *raised* again for our justification (Rom. 4:25).

> **Not to all the people, but unto witnesses chosen before of God, even to us, who did eat and drink with him after he rose from the dead.**

> **And he commanded us to preach unto the people, and to testify that it is he which was ordained of God to be the Judge of quick and dead.**

> **To him give all the prophets witness, that through his name whosoever believeth in him shall receive remission of sins [Acts 10:41–43].**

You may remember that I have pointed out Peter's weaknesses and his faults. I actually rejoice in the fact that Peter was so human and so like another fellow I know very well by the name of McGee. But the important thing is that Peter preached the Gospel. Here is the Gospel: Jesus Christ died, He has risen, and whoever believes in Him shall receive remission of sins. If we do not tell people that message, we are not telling them the Gospel.

> **While Peter yet spake these words, the Holy Ghost fell on all them which heard the word.**

And they of the circumcision which believed were astonished, as many as came with Peter, because that on the Gentiles also was poured out the gift of the Holy Ghost.

For they heard them speak with tongues, and magnify God. Then answered Peter,

Can any man forbid water, that these should not be baptized, which have received the Holy Ghost as well as we?

And he commanded them to be baptized in the name of the Lord. Then prayed they him to tarry certain days [Acts 10:44–48].

This incident has been called the Gentile Pentecost. Peter was astonished that the Gentiles should receive the Holy Spirit. This outpouring of the Holy Spirit was made audible by their speaking in tongues. The tongues were an evidence to Simon Peter and the others with him that God would save the Gentiles and would give to them His Holy Spirit. Peter later relates this evidence that these Gentiles had believed on the Lord Jesus Christ and that God had granted repentance unto life also to the Gentiles (Acts 11:17–18). In Acts 15:7–11 Peter again refers to this incident, declaring that it proves that the Holy Ghost has been given to the Gentiles and that they are saved through the grace of the Lord Jesus Christ just as are the Jews. It is hard for us to realize the great barrier that existed between Jew and Gentile. The Jews of that day simply could not believe that Gentiles were going to be saved—in spite of the fact that the Lord had told them this was to be so. Then the Gentiles at Cornelius' house are baptized in water.

Again let me call your attention to the fact that the Book of Acts records three representative conversions. The Ethiopian eunuch was a son of Ham. Saul of Tarsus was a son of Shem. Cornelius was a son of Japheth. In each instance the Holy Spirit moved, using a man of God and the Word of God.

CHAPTER 11

THEME: Peter defends his ministry; Gospel goes to Antioch

Peter recounts the events in connection with the conversion of Gentiles in the home of Cornelius. The news that the Gentiles had received the Word of God did not seem to bring any joy to the church in Jerusalem. They demand of Peter an explanation of his conduct, so Peter must defend his ministry—which is really difficult for Simon Peter, as he himself feels apologetic about it.

Antioch becomes the center of the gentile church.

PETER DEFENDS HIS MINISTRY

And the apostles and brethren that were in Judaea heard that the Gentiles had also received the word of God.

And when Peter was come up to Jerusalem, they that were of the circumcision contended with him,

Saying, Thou wentest in to men uncircumcised, and didst eat with them [Acts 11:1–3].

There was doubt and division. We need to understand that to the Jews the action of Simon Peter was a terrible thing. In fact, if we could have talked to Simon Peter a month before this, he also would have said it was a terrible thing to do. Actually, Peter gives them an apology. He makes it clear that he didn't want to do it at all, but that the Spirit of God was in the whole episode.

But Peter rehearsed the matter from the beginning, and expounded it by order unto them, saying,

I was in the city of Joppa praying: and in a trance I saw a vision, A certain vessel descend, as it had been a great sheet, let down from heaven by four corners; and it came even to me:

Upon the which when I had fastened mine eyes, I considered, and saw fourfooted beasts of the earth, and wild beasts, and creeping things, and fowls of the air [Acts 11:4–6].

Listen to his account. He is still amazed at God's command.

And I heard a voice saying unto me, Arise, Peter; slay and eat.

But I said, Not so, Lord: for nothing common or unclean hath at any time entered into my mouth.

But the voice answered me again from heaven, What God hath cleansed, that call not thou common.

And this was done three times: and all were drawn up again into heaven [Acts 11:7–10].

The word for "drawn up" indicates all were suddenly withdrawn into heaven.

And, behold, immediately there were three men already come unto the house where I was, sent from Caesarea unto me.

And the Spirit bade me go with them, nothing doubting. Moreover these six brethren accompanied me, and we entered into the man's house:

And he shewed us how he had seen an angel in his house, which stood and said unto him, Send men to Joppa, and call for Simon, whose surname is Peter;

> Who shall tell thee words, whereby thou and all thy
> house shall be saved.

> And as I began to speak, the Holy Ghost fell on them, as
> on us at the beginning [Acts 11:11-15].

Now Simon Peter tells what went through his mind.

> Then remembered I the word of the Lord, how that he
> said, John indeed baptized with water; but ye shall be
> baptized with the Holy Ghost.

> Forasmuch then as God gave them the like gift as he did
> unto us, who believed on the Lord Jesus Christ; what
> was I, that I could withstand God? [Acts 11:16-17].

The purpose of the tongues was to give evidence to Simon Peter that
the Holy Spirit had actually "fallen on them." How else would he have
known that they had been baptized by the Holy Spirit which placed
them in the body of believers?

> When they heard these things, they held their peace,
> and glorified God, saying, Then hath God also to the
> Gentiles granted repentance unto life [Acts 11:18].

Even the Judaizers had to shut their mouths now. They had nothing
more to say in objection because this obviously was of God. So they
glorified God. This was a great day—the door had been opened to the
Gentiles! We see now that the stage is being set for the Gospel to move
out to the ends of the earth.

GOSPEL GOES TO ANTIOCH

> Now they which were scattered abroad upon the perse-
> cution that arose about Stephen travelled as far as Phe-
> nice, and Cyprus, and Antioch, preaching the word to
> none but unto the Jews only.

> And some of them were men of Cyprus and Cyrene,
> which, when they were come to Antioch, spake unto the
> Grecians, preaching the Lord Jesus [Acts 11:19–20].

The "Grecians," you will remember, are Jews who spoke Greek and were Greek in their customs. So far, you will notice, the preaching has been to Jews only.

> And the hand of the Lord was with them: and a great
> number believed, and turned unto the Lord.
>
> Then tidings of these things came unto the ears of the
> church which was in Jerusalem: and they sent forth
> Barnabas, that he should go as far as Antioch [Acts
> 11:21–22].

There is a great moving of the Spirit of God in Antioch, and the church in Jerusalem hears about it. So the Jerusalem church sends Barnabas to Antioch. We are going to see now that Antioch becomes the second center of the church. In fact, the center actually shifts from Jerusalem to Antioch.

> Who, when he came, and had seen the grace of God,
> was glad, and exhorted them all, that with purpose of
> heart they would cleave unto the Lord.
>
> For he was a good man, and full of the Holy Ghost and of
> faith: and much people was added unto the Lord [Acts
> 11:23–24].

This is a wonderful thing that is said about Barnabas. He was a good man, full of the Holy Spirit, and full of faith. And, my friend, there is no reason why every Christian shouldn't be a good person.

Barnabas became the pastor of the church there. He began "exhorting," which would be preaching and teaching. And the congregation grew, for "much people was added unto the Lord." As the church grew, it became evident to Barnabas that he needed an assistant pastor, and he knew where to get a good one.

Then departed Barnabas to Tarsus, for to seek Saul:

And when he had found him, he brought him unto Antioch. And it came to pass, that a whole year they assembled themselves with the church, and taught much people. And the disciples were called Christians first in Antioch [Acts 11:25–26].

Barnabas had to go find Saul and bring him with him. I detect in this that Saul was a little reluctant to come. He held back.

It was here that believers in the Lord Jesus Christ were first called "Christians." I do not think this was a term of ridicule. I think it simply meant that these were the ones who were the followers of Christ; they were *Christians*. It is an excellent name.

And in these days came prophets from Jerusalem unto Antioch.

And there stood up one of them named Agabus, and signified by the spirit that there should be great dearth throughout all the world: which came to pass in the days of Claudius Caesar.

Then the disciples, every man according to his ability, determined to send relief unto the brethren which dwelt in Judaea:

Which also they did, and sent it to the elders by the hands of Barnabas and Saul [Acts 11:27–30].

The incident that is recorded here is also verified in secular history. There was a general famine, but the effect was especially felt in Jerusalem where the church had been persecuted, decimated, and hurt. They were in dire need during this time. It is wonderful to see the fraternal spirit, the bond of love, that held the early church together. The other believers sent help to the troubled church in Jerusalem.

We remember that Saul had been one of those who had wasted the church in Jerusalem by his relentless persecution of them. How wonderful it is to see that by his own hands a transformed Saul now brings *relief* to that same church. That is Christianity in shoe leather, my friend. That is the way it ought to be.

CHAPTER 12

THEME: Death of James; arrest of Peter

In this chapter persecution strikes through Herod Agrippa I. James is executed and Peter is imprisoned—but is miraculously delivered. Herod dies by a judgment of God. Although persecution comes, the church grows and the Word of God is multiplied.

DEATH OF JAMES

Now about that time Herod the king stretched forth his hands to vex certain of the church [Acts 12:1].

"Herod the king" is Herod Agrippa I, grandson of Herod the Great (who attempted to put the Lord Jesus to death at the time of His birth). There never was a family more at enmity against God. As far as we know, not a single member of the Herod family ever really turned to God.

You will recall that up to this point the persecution against the church had been largely from the religious rulers, the Sadducees in particular. Now it moves into the realm of government. Persecution swings from religion to politics. Perhaps Herod did this to gain favor with certain influential groups. We know that he stretched forth his hands to vex certain of the church. The word *vexed* is hardly adequate to describe what he did. He carried on a brutal, unfeeling persecution of the church.

And he killed James the brother of John with the sword [Acts 12:2].

The fact is stated so bluntly—he killed James with the sword. James becomes another martyr in the church. He is the second martyr who is named. I am of the opinion that there had been many others who had already died for the name of the Lord Jesus.

> **And because he saw it pleased the Jews, he proceeded further to take Peter also. (Then were the days of unleavened bread.) [Acts 12:3].**

James is slain, but Peter will be miraculously preserved in all of this. Here we find an example of the sovereign will of God moving in the church. I'm sure there were many who asked, "Why in the world was James put to death and Peter permitted to live? Why would God do that?" Many ask that same question today. The answer is that this is the sovereign will of God. He still moves like this in the contemporary church. I have been in the ministry for many years, and I have seen the Lord reach in and take certain wonderful members out of the church by death. And then there are others whom He has left. Why would He do that? If He had asked me, from my viewpoint as the pastor, I would say that He took the wrong one and He left the wrong one! But life and death are in the hands of a sovereign God. When you and I rebel against His decision, it is simply too bad for us. This is His universe, not ours. It is God's church, not ours. The hand of a sovereign God moves in the church.

James apparently was one of the heads of the church in Jerusalem. God permits Herod to slay him. Peter must have been a leader too. God permits him to live.

> **And when he had apprehended him, he put him in prison, and delivered him to four quaternions of soldiers to keep him; intending after Easter to bring him forth to the people [Acts 12:4].**

The word *Easter* should be "Passover." Actually, they are at the same time because you remember that Jesus ate the meal with His disciples just before He was crucified. However, the Jews in Jerusalem at this time would have been celebrating the Passover and not Easter.

He really put Peter under guard here. The guard is strengthened and enlarged. *Four quaternions* of soldiers to keep this man! Wouldn't you say that he suspected someone would try to deliver Peter?

PETER'S DELIVERANCE

Peter therefore was kept in prison: but prayer was made without ceasing of the church unto God for him [Acts 12:5].

Another translation would be "but prayer was made earnestly of the church unto God for him." They didn't come before God with a kind of grocery-list prayer. They went before God and earnestly prayed that this man Simon Peter be delivered. Their hearts were in their prayers.

And when Herod would have brought him forth, the same night Peter was sleeping between two soldiers, bound with two chains: and the keepers before the door kept the prison [Acts 12:6].

How could Simon Peter sleep between two soldiers? Remember that he went to sleep also in the Garden of Gethsemane. I would say that Simon Peter was not troubled with insomnia. He didn't have any difficulty sleeping. It seems he could sleep just about any place and any time. What a wonderful confidence he must have had in God to be able to sleep between these two soldiers!

And, behold, the angel of the Lord came upon him, and a light shined in the prison: and he smote Peter on the side, and raised him up, saying, Arise up quickly. And his chains fell off from his hands.

And the angel said unto him, Gird thyself, and bind on thy sandals. And so he did. And he saith unto him, Cast thy garment about thee, and follow me.

And he went out, and followed him; and wist not that it was true which was done by the angel; but thought he saw a vision [Acts 12:7–9].

The angel tells him to do a very reasonable thing—get dressed. There was nothing in the way of alarm, just sensible directions. Peter thought the whole thing was a dream, and he would have walked out of there without his shoes!

> When they were past the first and the second ward, they came unto the iron gate that leadeth unto the city; which opened to them of his own accord: and they went out, and passed on through one street; and forthwith the angel departed from him [Acts 12:10].

They certainly had enough guards to keep Peter in prison. I really think that they expected something like this. You remember that the Lord Jesus had come forth from the grave. That was a source of real embarrassment to them. They do not intend to let something like that happen to them again. So they more than doubled the guard.

Remember that the church in Jerusalem is praying for Simon Peter while this is happening. As soon as Peter is out of danger, the angel lets Peter go on his own.

Let me call attention to the fact that the translation in verse 7 should be *an* angel of the Lord and not *the* angel of the Lord. The angel of the Lord in the Old Testament referred to the preincarnate Christ. Jesus Christ is now at God's right hand in His glorified body. It was not the Lord Jesus who came down to deliver Peter. It was an angel whom the Lord Jesus had sent. The prayers of the church are definitely answered.

> And when Peter was come to himself, he said, Now I know of a surety, that the Lord hath sent his angel, and hath delivered me out of the hand of Herod, and from all the expectation of the people of the Jews [Acts 12:11].

Peter immediately recognizes that God has delivered him.

> And when he had considered the thing, he came to the house of Mary the mother of John, whose surname was

**Mark; where many were gathered together praying
[Acts 12:12].**

The church at this particular time, and for about a hundred and fifty
years after this, did not have church buildings. Today, when we talk of
a church, we usually mean a building. We say, "The First So-and-So
church is on the corner of Main and So-and-So." Actually, that is not a
church at all; it is a building in which the church meets. The church is
the body of believers. At the beginning the church never met in a public buildings. They had none. They met in homes.

Now Mary, the mother of John Mark, apparently was a woman of
means and had a home large enough for the church to meet there. They
were gathered together praying for Simon Peter to be delivered.

**And as Peter knocked at the door of the gate, a damsel
came to hearken, named Rhoda [Acts 12:13].**

"To hearken" means that she came to the door to listen. These were
days of persecution. It was important to know who was knocking.
Rhoda means "rose"; she was probably a servant girl.

**And when she knew Peter's voice, she opened not the
gate for gladness, but ran in, and told how Peter stood
before the gate [Acts 12:14].**

She forgot all about opening the gate, you see. She was so excited that
she just left him standing there at the gate while she rushed back to the
people who were praying.

**And they said unto her, Thou art mad. But she con-
stantly affirmed that it was even so. Then said they, It is
his angel [Acts 12:15].**

When she tells them Peter is at the gate, they tell her she is crazy. "No,"
she tells them, "Peter is at the gate." "Well, did you see him?" "No, I

didn't open the gate, but I heard him and I know his voice." "Oh," they say, "it's his spirit." The word *angel* is *pneuma*, which really means "spirit" rather than angel. They are not saying that he has a guardian angel. They think it is his spirit. In other words, they think Peter is dead, that he has been slain by Herod.

It is interesting that while the Jesus is praying for Simon Peter to be delivered, he is delivered; but when it happens, they don't believe it. They think he has been slain, and it is his spirit which has appeared.

It is a great comfort to me that the early church, with all of its tremendous spiritual power, did not believe that their prayers had been answered on this occasion. They didn't believe that Simon Peter had actually been delivered. Isn't that same thing true of us so many times? When we do have an answer to our prayer, we rejoice and talk about it as if we are really surprised. And we are surprised—to be honest, we really didn't expect an answer. Yet God heard and answered our prayer. How gracious He is!

"But Peter continued knocking." That's just like Peter. Nobody's opening the gate because they don't believe their prayers have been answered—they are in there arguing whether it is Peter or whether it is his spirit. Peter wants in and he is about to knock that gate down!

But Peter continued knocking: and when they had opened the door, and saw him, they were astonished.

But he, beckoning unto them with the hand to hold their peace, declared unto them how the Lord had brought him out of the prison. And he said, Go shew these things unto James, and to the brethren. And he departed, and went into another place [Acts 12:16–17].

They just couldn't believe their eyes. They just couldn't believe that their prayers had been answered.

Now Peter got out of town. Since God had miraculously delivered him, couldn't God have miraculously kept him safe in Jerusalem? Shouldn't Peter have said, "I'm just going to stick around. God has delivered me out of prison, and I know He can keep me"? Of course, God could keep him. But God expects us to use our common sense.

Sometimes what looks like a tremendous faith in God is actually tempting God. Even after God has done some wonderful or miraculous thing for you and for me, He still expects us to use our common sense.

Now as soon as it was day, there was no small stir among the soldiers, what was become of Peter [Acts 12:18].

Notice that Dr. Luke uses the diminutive—"no small stir." When he says there was no small stir, believe me, he means there was a mighty big stir. Also in chapter 15 of Acts, when Judaism came into the church, Dr. Luke says they had "no small dissension." He means they had a regular knock-down-drag-out. They had a real fight, a regular donnybrook. But Dr. Luke always uses that very gracious and gentle diminutive—"no small stir" and "no small dissension."

When the soldiers found what had happened and realized that Simon Peter was gone, I think they called out half the army. They must have made a house-to-house search. Maybe they threw a guard around the city to prevent his escape. There was no small stir according to Dr. Luke. I'll say not! There was a mighty big stir.

And when Herod had sought for him, and found him not, he examined the keepers, and commanded that they should be put to death. And he went down from Judaea to Caesarea, and there abode [Acts 12:19].

Herod is cold-blooded and he is hardhearted. He has no regard for human life. By executing the guards, he is saying to the world that he does not believe Peter's escape was an act of God. He is holding his men responsible. He executes all the soldiers who were guarding Peter. Then he goes down to Caesarea, which is a resort area on the Mediterranean. Pilate enjoyed it down there, and many of the Roman rulers stayed down there. Actually, it was the Roman headquarters. Romans, like Pilate, didn't care for Jerusalem. They certainly didn't love Jerusalem as king David had. So now Herod beats it down to Caesarea to have a little vacation.

DEATH OF HEROD

Now we will see that God holds Herod responsible for the light He has given him.

> **And Herod was highly displeased with them of Tyre and Sidon: but they came with one accord to him, and, having made Blastus the king's chamberlain their friend, desired peace; because their country was nourished by the king's country [Acts 12:20].**

Tyre and Sidon did business with Herod and when he was displeased, this hurt the economy of Tyre and Sidon. So they came down to make an overture to Herod.

> **And upon a set day Herod, arrayed in royal apparel, sat upon his throne, and made an oration unto them [Acts 12:21].**

Herod was pompous and lifted up by pride. He was also a pleasing speaker. He was the kind of politician who would have been elected no matter what party he would run for.

Herod is one of the men who is a miniature of Antichrist. John tells us this in 1 John 2:18: "Little children, it is the last time: and as ye have heard that antichrist shall come, even now are there many antichrists; whereby we know that it is the last time." The people hail him as a deity.

> **And the people gave a shout, saying, It is the voice of a god, and not of a man.**
>
> **And immediately the angel of the Lord smote him, because he gave not God the glory: and he was eaten of worms, and gave up the ghost [Acts 12:22–23].**

Friend, God will not share His glory with anyone. "I am the LORD: that is my name: and my glory will I not give to another, neither my praise to graven images" (Isa. 42:8). Herod refused to glorify God through the miracle of Peter's escape from prison. And now he is willing to let the people deify *him!* God judges him. God is jealous of His glory. What a lesson we have here!

Now one would think that with all this persecution taking place the poor church would be destroyed and disappear.

But the word of God grew and multiplied [Acts 12:24].

Persecution didn't hurt the church at all.

And Barnabas and Saul returned from Jerusalem, when they had fulfilled their ministry, and took with them John, whose surname was Mark [Acts 12:25].

John Mark goes back to Antioch with Barnabas and Saul. Remember that they had been down in Jerusalem with the gift to the church there.

We have come now to the end of the second period of the Book of Acts. The Gospel has gone into Judea and Samaria. Beginning with the next chapter we will see the movement of the Gospel to the uttermost part of the earth. We are still in that movement today. I hope that you and I are both involved in it.

CHAPTERS 13 AND 14

THEME: First missionary journey of Paul

We come now to the final major division of the Book of Acts. It is the Lord Jesus Christ at work by the Holy Spirit through the apostles to the uttermost part of the earth. The section includes chapters 13—28.

You will remember that the key to the book is the fact that Jesus said, ". . . ye shall be witnesses unto me . . ." (Acts 1:8). This was not a command to the church as a corporate body but to you and me individually. This witness was to go out to Jerusalem, then to Judea and Samaria, and then to the uttermost part of the earth. During the Jerusalem period we saw that the Gospel went to the Jews, and the church was 100 percent Jewish—no Gentiles. During the next period we saw the Gospel go to the Samaritans and we saw the conversion of some Gentiles. Now the Gospel moves out officially on its way to the ends of the earth.

On its way to the ends of the earth the Gospel came to my ancestors and to your ancestors. Today you and I are the beneficiaries of the fact that someone went down the road of this world to bring the Gospel to the ends of the earth. You and I ought to be in the business of taking the Gospel down beyond where we are to some who have not heard.

In this surge of the Gospel beyond the boundaries of Simon Peter we find that Paul becomes the dominant leader and Peter disappears from the scene. God had used him mightily. Now Paul is the dominant one whom God will use.

As you will see by the map, Paul begins his journey with Barnabas. The first stop is the island of Cyprus, the home of Barnabas. They cross the island, then set sail from Paphos to go over to Perga in Pamphylia. Then they enter the interior of Asia Minor, which is now Turkey, and go into the Galatian country. They visit Antioch, Iconium, Lystra, and Derbe; then they return through Attalia, and then sail back to Antioch.

BARNABAS AND PAUL SENT OUT FROM ANTIOCH

Now there were in the church that was at Antioch certain prophets and teachers; as Barnabas, and Simeon that was called Niger, and Lucius of Cyrene, and Manaen, which had been brought up with Herod the tetrarch, and Saul.

As they ministered to the Lord, and fasted, the Holy Ghost said, Separate me Barnabas and Saul for the work whereunto I have called them [Acts 13:1-2].

You will notice as they begin their ministry it is "Barnabas and Saul." They will not be very far into the first missionary journey until Saul's name is changed to Paul. It is soon evident that Paul becomes the leader and the chief spokesman; then this team is called "Paul and Barnabas."

And when they had fasted and prayed, and laid their hands on them, they sent them away [Acts 13:3].

These men are now set aside as missionaries. Did you notice the church that sent them forth into the world? It was not the church in Jerusalem. I say to you very candidly, the church in Jerusalem was not a missionary church. The church in Antioch had the missionary vision. They fasted and prayed because of their earnestness and their desire for the will of God.

They laid their hands on these two missionaries they were sending out. We still do that today to our missionaries. Why? Is it that we are imparting something to them? I'm afraid all that we can impart to someone by laying our hands on them is whatever disease germ we have on our hands. The laying on of hands is a means of identifying, of declaring that we are partners with that one. So the Christians in Antioch are indicating by placing their hands on them that they are in a partnership with Paul and Barnabas in the enterprise of getting out the Word of God. They are sending these men out as their representatives.

They will minister at home while Paul and Barnabas go to the regions beyond.

> So they, being sent forth by the Holy Ghost, departed
> unto Seleucia; and from thence they sailed to Cyprus
> [Acts 13:4].

The important thing is that they are sent forth by the Holy Spirit. They will be led by the Holy Spirit of God. They went down to the seacoast town of Seleucia and sailed from there.

> And when there at Salamis, they preached the word of
> God in the synagogues of the Jews: and they had also
> John to their ministry [Acts 13:5].

Notice that they had John Mark along with them.

From the very beginning Paul adopts a method which he followed through his entire ministry. He always used the Jewish synagogue as the springboard from which he preached the Gospel. A friend of mine was criticized for going to speak in a synagogue. This man preached the Gospel, I can assure you. I reminded his critic that Paul always went first to the synagogue to preach. If he was going to find fault with my friend, he would also have to find fault with the method of the apostle Paul.

OPPOSITION AT PAPHOS

> And when they had gone through the isle unto Paphos,
> they found a certain sorcerer, a false prophet, a Jew,
> whose name was Bar-jesus [Acts 13:6].

It would appear that their ministry didn't have much success at Salamis. At least no record is given of any fruit from their ministry. They cross over the Isle of Cyprus to the other side of the island. In Paphos they encounter this opposition, which is actually satanic, through a sorcerer who had a tremendous influence on the Roman deputy, the governor of that island, Sergius Paulus.

> **Which was with the deputy of the country, Sergius Paulus, a prudent man; who called for Barnabas and Saul, and desired to hear the word of God.**

> **But Elymas the sorcerer (for so is his name by interpretation) withstood them, seeking to turn away the deputy from the faith [Acts 13:7–8].**

This is satanic opposition. This man had the governor under his influence. Unfortunately there are a great many rulers today who are under the influence of all kinds of cultism which is in opposition to the Word of God and in opposition to the Gospel.

> **Then Saul (who also is called Paul,) filled with the Holy Ghost, set his eyes on him [Acts 13:9].**

Here his name is changed. Why was he called Paul? The name *Paul* means "small or little." Some think that he took that name as an act of humility, that he no longer wanted to bear the proud name of Saul. It is possible he took the name of the governor, Sergius Paulus, who was his first convert.

> **And said, O full of all subtilty and all mischief, thou child of the devil, thou enemy of all righteousness, wilt thou not cease to pervert the right ways of the Lord? [Acts 13:10].**

Paul may have been a mild man in some ways, but I tell you, when he encountered this kind of opposition, he denounced it with all his being. He recognized it as satanic and he denounced it. I think we ought to do the same today.

> And now, behold, the hand of the Lord is upon thee, and
> thou shalt be blind, not seeing the sun for a season. And
> immediately there fell on him a mist and a darkness;
> and he went about seeking some to lead him by the hand
> [Acts 13:11].

He was already in spiritual darkness. Now he is put into physical darkness as well.

> Then the deputy, when he saw what was done, believed,
> being astonished at the doctrine of the Lord [Acts
> 13:12].

I call your attention to the fact that Paul had the sign gifts of an apostle. When he went over there to Paphos, he couldn't ask them to turn to the New Testament. There was no New Testament for him to preach from or for them to turn to. He couldn't preach from the Epistle to the Romans because he hadn't written it yet. They couldn't turn to the Gospel of John because John hadn't written it yet. So how will they recognize his authority? It is by the sign gifts. Today, the New Testament is written. We are now given a different way to recognize authority. "If there come any unto you, and bring not this doctrine, receive him not into your house, neither bid him God speed" (2 John 10). This doctrine is in the Word of God, in the New Testament.

Probably the sorcerer had been doing some fancy tricks by the power of Satan. In that day a false prophet could probably heal and perform other miracles by the power of Satan.

Paul has his authority from the Lord Jesus Christ. He absolutely dominates the sorcerer by his message of the Gospel of the Lord Jesus Christ. Sergius Paulus comes to the light. He has been in spiritual darkness but now believes and is astonished at the doctrine of the Lord.

> Now when Paul and his company loosed from Paphos,
> they came to Perga in Pamphylia: and John departing
> from them returned to Jerusalem [Acts 13:13].

That is all Dr. Luke says; he mildly records the fact of John Mark's departure. He doesn't issue a tirade against him. We will learn later that John Mark actually deserted. He showed a yellow streak and ran home to mommy. Remember that his mother was a prominent member of the church in Jerusalem and that her home was the place of meeting for the church there. When he reached Perga and got a look into the interior of Asia Minor—the paganism and the physical dangers and hardships that were there—he decided that he hadn't been called as a missionary. He heads in another direction, and that direction is home.

Later on we find that Paul refuses to take John Mark on another missionary journey. In fact, Paul and Barnabas finally separated. Paul went one way and Barnabas went another way. Paul was wrong about John Mark. God didn't throw him overboard because of his failure. Thank God, He doesn't throw us overboard because of our failure either. He gave John Mark another chance. Later on Paul was big enough to admit he had been wrong, and when he was close to his death, he actually asked for John Mark to come to him. "Only Luke is with me. Take Mark, and bring him with thee: for he is profitable to me for the ministry" (2 Tim. 4:11). This is the John Mark who wrote the Gospel of Mark. He made good. Thank God. He gives us a second chance!

However here at the beginning John Mark is a failure. He left them and returned to Jerusalem. Meanwhile Paul and Barnabas go into the interior of Asia Minor.

PAUL'S SERMON AT ANTIOCH

But when they departed from Perga, they came to Antioch in Pisidia, and went into the synagogue on the sabbath day, and sat down.

And after the reading of the law and the prophets the rulers of the synagogue sent unto them, saying, Ye men and brethren, if ye have any word of exhortation for the people, say on [Acts 13:14–15].

Paul follows his method of going first to the synagogue. Jews were scattered throughout the Roman Empire, and they established syna-

gogues in the cities in which they had settled. When visitors would
come from Jerusalem, since they would want word from the religious
center, they would invite the visitor to say something. This always af-
forded a marvelous opportunity for the apostle Paul. He certainly took
advantage of it here.

This sermon which Paul preached in Antioch of Pisidia is one of
the great sermons, in my opinion; yet it is generally passed by today. It
is the first recorded sermon on Paul, preached in the synagogue on the
Sabbath day. When they asked Paul whether he would like to say something, you can be sure that he wanted to say something. That was his
whole reason for being there.

> **Then Paul stood up, and beckoning with his hand said,
> Men of Israel, and ye that fear God, give audience [Acts
> 13:16].**

One would conclude from this introduction that there were some visitors there—probably Gentile proselytes.

> **The God of this people of Israel chose our fathers, and
> exalted the people when they dwelt as strangers in the
> land of Egypt, and with an high arm brought he them
> out of it.**
>
> **And about the time of forty years suffered he their man-
> ners in the wilderness.**
>
> **And when he had destroyed seven nations in the land of
> Chanaan, he divided their land to them by lot.**
>
> **And after that he gave unto them judges about the space
> of four hundred and fifty years, until Samuel the
> prophet [Acts 13:17–20].**

Notice that Paul is doing the same thing that Stephen did before the
Sanhedrin. He recounts Israel's history as a nation.

And afterward they desired a king: and God gave unto them Saul the son of Cis, a man of the tribe of Benjamin, by the space of forty years.

And when he had removed him, he raised up unto them David to be their king; to whom also he gave testimony, and said, I have found David the son of Jesse, a man after mine own heart, which shall fulfil all my will.

Of this man's seed hath God according to his promise raised unto Israel a Saviour, Jesus [Acts 13:21–23].

After recounting their history, he will present to them the person of the Savior.

When John had first preached before his coming the baptism of repentance to all the people of Israel.

And as John fulfilled his course, he said, Whom think ye that I am? I am not he. But, behold, there cometh one after me, whose shoes of his feet I am not worthy to loose.

Men and brethren, children of the stock of Abraham, and whosoever among you feareth God, to you is the word of this salvation sent [Acts 13:24–26].

These people apparently had heard of John the Baptist. Now Paul will get down to the nitty-gritty.

For they that dwell at Jerusalem, and their rulers, because they knew him not, nor yet the voices of the prophets which are read every sabbath day, they have fulfilled them in condemning him.

And though they found no cause of death in him, yet desired they Pilate that he should be slain [Acts 13:27–28].

As Paul is reviewing their history, he is pointing out that all this was done as a fulfillment of prophecy. They were fulfilling the prophets at the very same time they were reading them! They read without understanding what they were reading.

> **And when they had fulfilled all that was written of him, they took him down from the tree, and laid him in a sepulchre.**
>
> **But God raised him from the dead:**
>
> **And he was seen many days of them which came up with him from Galilee to Jerusalem, who are his witnesses unto the people [Acts 13:29–31].**

You will notice that the core, the heart of every sermon preached in the New Testament, is the death and resurrection of Jesus Christ. That is the message. Simon Peter preached it; now Paul the apostle preaches it. There is not the slightest disagreement in the message of these two men. Don't tell me these two men disagreed. They did not!

> **And we declare unto you glad tidings, how that the promise which was made unto the fathers,**
>
> **God hath fulfilled the same unto us their children, in that he hath raised up Jesus again; as it is also written in the second pslam, Thou art my Son, this day have I begotten thee [Acts 13:32–33].**

This Old Testament reference, Psalm 2:7, does not refer to the birth of Christ; it refers to the resurrection of Christ. "This day have I begotten thee"—not begotten in the Virgin Birth but actually in the resurrection from the dead.

> **And as concerning that he raised him up from the dead, now no more to return to corruption, he said on this wise, I will give you the sure mercies of David.**

> Wherefore he saith also in another psalm, Thou shalt
> not suffer thine Holy One to see corruption [Acts
> 13:34-35].

Paul enlarges upon the Resurrection. He is citing the same that Simon
Peter did on the Day of Pentecost.

> For David, after he had served his own generation by the
> will of God, fell on sleep, and was laid unto his fathers,
> and saw corruption:
>
> But he, whom God raised again, saw no corruption.
>
> Be it known unto you therefore, men and brethren, that
> through this man is preached unto you the forgiveness
> of sins:
>
> And by him all that believe are justified from all things,
> from which ye could not be justified by the law of Moses
> [Acts 13:36-39].

Now he is pinning this thing down. He is explaining the significance
of the death and resurrection of Jesus Christ. He is actually asking
them for a decision to believe on the Lord Jesus.

> Beware therefore, lest that come upon you, which is spo-
> ken of in the prophets;
>
> Behold, ye despisers, and wonder, and perish: for I
> work a work in your days, a work which ye shall in no
> wise believe, though a man declare it unto you [Acts
> 13:40-41].

Here is his appeal to them. He urges them not to reject the message.

> And when the Jews were gone out of the synagogue, the
> Gentiles besought that these words might be preached to
> them the next sabbath [Acts 13:42].

There were Gentiles there who said, "We would like to hear this same message."

> Now when the congregation was broken up, many of the Jews and religious proselytes followed Paul and Barnabas: who, speaking to them, persuaded them to continue in the grace of God.

> And the next sabbath day came almost the whole city together to hear the word of God [Acts 13:43–44].

There must have been much discussion of Paul's message. The next Sabbath day almost the entire city was there to hear Paul preach.

> But when the Jews saw the multitudes, they were filled with envy, and spake against those things which were spoken by Paul, contradicting and blaspheming [Acts 13:45].

This time there was a big commotion because the leading religious rulers of the synagogue opposed Paul and Barnabas.

> Then Paul and Barnabas waxed bold, and said, It was necessary that the word of God should first have been spoken to you: but seeing ye put it from you, and judge yourselves unworthy of everlasting life, lo, we turn to the Gentiles.

> For so hath the Lord commanded us, saying, I have set thee to be a light of the Gentiles, that thou shouldest be for salvation unto the ends of the earth.

> And when the Gentiles heard this, they were glad, and glorified the word of the Lord: and as many as were ordained to eternal life believed.

> And the word of the Lord was published throughout all the region [Acts 13:46–49].

Here is the recurring pattern. The Gospel is preached to the Jews first; they reject it; so they turn to the Gentiles with the good news.

But the Jews stirred up the devout and honourable women, and the chief men of the city, and raised persecution against Paul and Barnabas, and expelled them out of their coasts [Acts 13:50].

They were run out of town; they actually were forced to leave the town.

But they shook off the dust of their feet against them, and came unto Iconium.

And the disciples were filled with joy, and with the Holy Ghost [Acts 13:51–52].

Notice the condition of those who were converted. They were filled with joy, and they were filled with the Holy Ghost.

GALATIAN COUNTRY

Now in chapter 14 Paul and Barnabas face the almost impenetrable paganism of Galatia. I personally believe that the Galatian field was the hardest mission field that Paul ever entered. You need only to read the Epistle to the Galatians to discover that. Galatians was the harshest epistle that Paul wrote. He wrote it to a group of people who had a spiritual bent in the wrong direction. They were constantly going off the track. He visited those churches more than any others.

Let me give you this brief background of the Galatian country which Paul is entering on this first missionary journey. The people for whom the province was named were Gauls, a Celtic tribe from the same stock which inhabited France. In the fourth century B.C. they invaded the Roman Empire and sacked Rome. Later they crossed into Greece and captured Delphi in 280 B.C. At the invitation of Nikomedes I, King of Bithynia, they crossed over into Asia Minor to help him in a civil war. They were a warlike people and soon established themselves in Asia Minor. In 189 B.C. they were made subjects of the Roman Empire and became a province. Their boundaries varied, and for many years they retained their customs and language. The churches which Paul established on this first missionary journey were included at one time in the territory of Galatia, so this is the name which Paul would normally give to these churches.

PAUL'S *FIRST* MISSIONARY JOURNEY

The people were blond orientals. These Galtic Celts had much of the same temperament and characteristics of the majority of the American population, which came out of that same stock in Europe and the British Isles. Caesar had this to say of them: "The infirmity of the Gauls is that they are fickle in their resolves, fond of change, and not to be trusted." Another writer of that period described them as "frank, impetuous, impressible, eminently intelligent, fond of show, but extremely inconstant, the fruit of excessive vanity." Paul wrote them a very harsh letter because they needed that kind of letter. The majority of the people in the United States are like them. That is the reason so many cults and "isms" have begun in this country. We are a fickle people. One day we follow one leader, and the next day we follow someone else. It is amazing to watch the polls of our political candidates. If they make one statement, one slip of the tongue, the entire population shifts from them to someone else. We are a fickle people—very much like the Galatians.

All of this should make this section especially interesting to us. Martin Luther used the Epistle to the Galatians for the Reformation because it was written to folk who are like we are.

THE WORK IN ICONIUM

And it came to pass in Iconium, that they went both together into the synagogue of the Jews, and so spake, that a great multitude both of the Jews and also of the Greeks believed [Acts 14:1].

If you follow the journey on a map, you will notice that they crossed over the length of the island of Cyprus, and then sailed to Perga in Pamphylia. Then they traveled up into the country of Antioch, Iconium, Lystra, and Derbe. These are the cities of Galatia. So they are now in the heartland of Asia Minor.

But the unbelieving Jews stirred up the Gentiles, and made their minds evil affected against the brethren.

Long time therefore abode they speaking boldly in the Lord, which gave testimony unto the word of his grace, and granted signs and wonders to be done by their hands.

But the multitude of the city was divided: and part held with the Jews, and part with the apostles [Acts 14:2–4].

Paul and Barnabas cause quite a division in the city. You must remember that Paul and Barnabas are both Jews. They always went to the Jews first and used the synagogue as a springboard to get to the Gentiles.

And when there was an assault made both of the Gentiles, and also of the Jews with their rulers, to use them despitefully, and to stone them,

They were ware of it, and fled unto Lystra and Derbe, cities of Lycaonia, and unto the region that lieth round about:

And there they preached the gospel [Acts 14:5–7].

Because they didn't get a very good reception in Iconium, they fled to Lystra and Derbe. However, we know that they came back through Iconium so there must have been some believers there.

THE EVENTS AT LYSTRA

And there sat a certain man at Lystra, impotent in his feet, being a cripple from his mother's womb, who never had walked:

The same heard Paul speak: who stedfastly beholding him, and perceiving that he had faith to be healed,

Said with a loud voice, Stand upright on thy feet. And he leaped and walked [Acts 14:8–10].

As we have seen, Paul and Barnabas had the gifts of an apostle, the sign gifts. They came into these places without any New Testament with the message of the Gospel. What were their credentials? How could they prove their message was from God? The sign gifts were their credentials—they needed them. Today we have the entire Bible, and what it has to say. If only we could get people to do that!

The other day I played golf with a very affable, generous, big-hearted man. He is an unsaved man, and he told me very candidly that he was chasing around. Mutual friends had asked me to play with him. I attempted to talk with him about the Gospel. He knew the facts of the Gospel as well as I do. And you know something else? He believed them. He said he believed that Jesus died and rose again, and he believed that if he put his trust in Jesus, He would save him. So I asked him why he didn't do that. Then he began to mention names, names of certain men whose lives just didn't measure up to their profession of faith. So I said to him, "For goodness sake get your eyes off men. In the first century the apostles performed miracles, and men got their eyes on the apostles. So it was necessary to get their eyes off the apostles and turn them to the Book which presents the Lord Jesus Christ. You need to get your eyes on the Word of God and learn what God says today. He tells us that the important thing is our personal relationship with God through Jesus Christ. All those other men you mention will not even enter into the picture when you stand before the Lord Jesus someday. The only question will be your personal relationship to Jesus Christ as it is revealed in the Word of God. Go to the Word of God." I'll be very frank with you; I didn't really get very far with this man. He did say that I had given him a new approach; he had never heard it that way before. He thought maybe he would try it. I encouraged him again to get his eyes off other Christians because we all have feet of clay.

The people at Lystra were looking to Paul and Barnabas.

> **And when the people saw what Paul had done, they lifted up their voices, saying in the speech of Lycaonia, The gods are come down to us in the likeness of men [Acts 14:11].**

The man had real faith to be healed. When Paul told him to stand up-right on his feet, he leaped and walked. Remember that the people in the area were pagan, heathen people. When they saw what Paul had done, they began to shout that the gods had come down in the likeness of men. Their eyes were on Paul and Barnabas. They were really ex-cited about them.

> **And they called Barnabas, Jupiter; and Paul, Mercu-rius, because he was the chief speaker.**

> **Then the priest of Jupiter, which was before their city, brought oxen and garlands unto the gates, and would have done sacrifice with the people [Acts 14:12–13].**

Paul is the leader of the team, the chief speaker, and the people want to make them gods. They bring garlands and sacrifice and are ready to worship them. Fickle! Does it remind you of someone else? In America it is a baseball player one year, then a politician, then a football star, then another politician. By the following year they are all forgotten, and it is someone else new. It is the same way with the preachers. One can preach the Word of God, and everyone will acclaim him as a wonderful preacher. Then the next day they are ready to crucify him.

> **Which when the apostles, Barnabas and Paul, heard of, they rent their clothes, and ran in among the people, crying out,**

> **And saying, Sirs, why do ye these things? We also are men of like passions with you, and preach unto you that ye should turn from these vanities unto the living God, which made heaven, and earth, and the sea, and all things that are therein:**

> **Who in times past suffered all nations to walk in their own ways [Acts 14:14–16].**

Paul and Barnabas are not only startled and amazed that these people want to worship them, but they are completely shocked. They rush in among them, shouting, "We are human beings like you are!" You will remember that Peter had to say the same thing to Cornelius when Cornelius bowed down to him to worship him.

Certainly none of us is to bow down to worship any man. A Christian is not to be so obsequious that he gets down to lick the boots of anyone. Unfortunately, even in Christian work, we find some people who want others to bow to them. How tragic that is.

> **Nevertheless he left not himself without witness, in that he did good, and gave us rain from heaven, and fruitful seasons, filling our hearts with food and gladness.**

> **And with these sayings scarce restrained they the people, that they had not done sacrifice unto them [Acts 14:17–18].**

He is attempting to turn their attention to the living God who is the Creator. He wants to draw them away from their heathen, pagan idols and the mythology of the Greeks.

> **And there came thither certain Jews from Antioch and Iconium, who persuaded the people, and, having stoned Paul, drew him out of the city, supposing he had been dead [Acts 14:19].**

How amazing this is. Such fickle people! One day they are ready to worship Paul and Barnabas as gods. The next day they stone Paul to death.

(How like Americans—we follow fads. One time it is the hula hoop. Then it is the miniskirt. We simply follow one fad after another.)

They stoned Paul and dragged him out of the city "supposing he had been dead." Do you think he was dead? I'll tell you what I think. I think he was dead. Later Paul writes of the experience he had: "I knew a man in Christ above fourteen years ago, (whether in the body, I cannot tell; or whether out of the body, I cannot tell: God knoweth;) such an one caught up to the third heaven. And I knew such a man, (whether in the body, or out of the body, I cannot tell: God knoweth;) How that he was caught up into paradise, and heard unspeakable words, which it is not lawful for a man to utter" (2 Cor. 12:2–4). Who was that man? It was Paul himself. "And lest I should be exalted above measure through the abundance of the revelations, there was given to me a thorn in the flesh, the messenger of Satan to buffet me, lest I should be exalted above measure" (2 Cor. 12:7). I don't think that crowd left him there half dead; I think they left him dead. I believe that God raised him from the dead.

Why would God permit this stoning? Galatians 6:7 tells us: "Be not deceived; God is not mocked: for whatsoever a man soweth, that shall he also reap." Paul reaped what he had sowed. He had ordered the stoning of Stephen. Maybe someone will object that now he is converted. Yes, but even after conversion we will reap whatsoever we have sown. This is a law of nature as well as a law operating in our lives. We shall reap whatever we sow. Because Saul took part in the stoning of Stephen, years later the same thing happened to him.

> Howbeit, as the disciples stood round about him, he rose up, and came into the city: and the next day he departed with Barnabas to Derbe [Acts 14:20].

This is miraculous. A man who has been stoned would be brutally wounded. Paul rose up, and the very next day he was able to travel. This is a miracle whether or not he was actually raised from the dead.

> And when they had preached the gospel to that city, and had taught many, they returned again to Lystra, and to Iconium, and Antioch,
>
> Confirming the souls of the disciples, and exhorting them to continue in the faith, and that we must through much tribulation enter into the kingdom of God [Acts 14:21–22].

If you are following the map, you will notice that Derbe is the pivotal point. It is the end of the line. At this point they turn back and retrace their steps through Lystra, Iconium, and Antioch.

> And when they had ordained them elders in every church, and had prayed with fasting, they commended them to the Lord, on whom they believed [Acts 14:23].

They return through Pisida and Pamphylia, and preached again in Perga. Then they go to Attalia, and sail from that port back to Antioch.

> And thence sailed to Antioch, from whence they had been recommended to the grace of God for the work which they fulfilled.
>
> And when they were come, and had gathered the church together, they rehearsed all that God had done with them, and how he had opened the door of faith unto the Gentiles.

And there they abode long time with the disciples [Acts 14:26-28].

Paul and Barnabas return to Antioch to give a report of the work because this is the church that had sent them out. They revealed that God had now definitely opened the door of the Gospel to Gentiles. When the Gospel started out, the churches were comprised entirely of Hebrews. Then they became partially Gentile. And now the Gospel is going definitely to the Gentiles. Now the churches in Asia Minor are comprised entirely of Gentiles. Although there may also have been some Jews in these churches, it seems that in most places the Jews rejected the Gospel and the Gentiles received it.

BIBLIOGRAPHY
(Recommended for Further Study)

Alexander, J. A. *The Acts of the Apostles.* Carlisle, Pennsylvania: The Banner of Truth Trust, 1875.

Conybeare, W. J. and Howson, J. S. *The Life and Epistles of St. Paul.* Grand Rapids, Michigan: William B. Eerdmans Pub. Co., 1855. (A classic work)

Eims, Leroy. *Disciples in Action.* Wheaton, Illinois: Victor Books, 1981.

Frank, Harry Thomas, editor. *Hammond's Atlas of the Bible Lands.* Wheaton, Illinois: Scripture Press Publications, 1977. (Inexpensive atlas with splendid maps)

Gaebelein, Arno C. *The Acts of the Apostles.* Neptune, New Jersey: Loizeaux Brothers, 1912. (A fine interpretation)

Heading, John. *Acts: A Study in New Testament Christianity.* Kansas City, Kansas: Walterick Publishers.

Hiebert, D. Edmond. *Personalities Around Paul.* Chicago, Illinois: Moody Press, 1973. (Rich studies of people in contact with the Apostle Paul)

Ironside, H. A. *Lectures on the Book of Acts.* Neptune, New Jersey: Loizeaux Brothers, 1943. (Especially good for young Christians)

Jensen, Irving L. *Acts: An Inductive Study.* Chicago, Illinois: Moody Press, 1968.

Kelly, William. *An Exposition of the Acts of the Apostles.* Addison, Illinois: Bible Truth Publishers, 1890.

Kent, Homer A., Jr. *Jerusalem to Rome: Studies in the Book of Acts.* Grand Rapids: Baker Book House, 1974. (A splendid work for individual or group study)

Morgan, G. Campbell. *The Acts of the Apostles.* Old Tappan, New Jersey: Fleming H. Revell Co., 1924.

Rackham, R. B. *The Acts of the Apostles.* Grand Rapids, Michigan: Baker Book House, 1901. (A detailed study)

Robertson, A. T. *Epochs in the Life of Paul.* Grand Rapids, Michigan: Baker Book House, 1909.

Ryrie, Charles D. *The Acts of the Apostles.* Chicago, Illinois: Moody Press, 1961. (A fine, inexpensive survey)

Scroggie, W. Graham. *The Acts of the Apostles.* Grand Rapids, Michigan: Zondervan Publishing House, n.d. (Splendid outlines)

Thomas, W. H. Griffith. *Outline Studies in the Acts of the Apostles.* Grand Rapids, Michigan: William B. Eerdmans Publishing Co., 1956.

Vaughan, Curtis. *Acts.* Grand Rapids, Michigan: Zondervan Publishing House, 1974.

Vos, Howard F. *Beginnings in Bible Archeology.* Chicago, Illinois: Moody Press, 1973.